Dangerous Persuaders

Louise Samways is a Melbourne psychologist who is a recognised expert in the fields of psychological healing and health. Following the publication of her last book, *Your Mindbody Energy*, in which she gave a brief outline of how cults manipulated people by misusing psychological techniques, she was contacted by many victims and their families. The evident need for more widespread information about how cults manage to recruit people, and how to escape from their influence, led her to write this book.

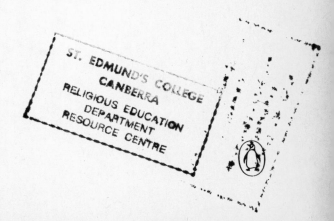

Dangerous Persuaders

An exposé of gurus, personal development courses and cults, and how they operate in Australia

LOUISE SAMWAYS

PENGUIN BOOKS

Penguin Books Australia Ltd
487 Maroondah Highway, PO Box 257
Ringwood, Victoria 3134, Australia
Penguin Books Ltd
Harmondsworth, Middlesex, England
Viking Penguin, A Division of Penguin Books USA Inc.
375 Hudson Street, New York, New York, 10014, USA
Penguin Books Canada Limited
10 Alcorn Avenue, Toronto, Ontario, Canada M4V 3B2
Penguin Books (N.Z.) Ltd
182-190 Wairau Road, Auckland 10, New Zealand

First published by Penguin Books Australia Ltd 1994

10 9 8 7 6 5 4 3 2

Produced by Viking O'Neil
56 Claremont Street, South Yarra, Victoria 3141, Australia
A Division of Penguin Books Australia Ltd

Typeset in 11pt Cheltenham by Midland Typesetters, Maryborough, Victoria 3465
Designed by George Dale
Printed in Australia by McPherson's Printing Group, Maryborough, Victoria 3465

National Library of Australia
Cataloguing-in-Publication data

Samways, Louise, 1951- .
Dangerous persuaders: an exposé of gurus, personal development courses and cults.

Bibliography.
ISBN 0 14 023553 1.

1. Cults-Australia. I. Title.

291

Contents

Preface

Dangerous Persuaders has evolved not from an academic study of cults and personal development courses, but from thousands of personal stories told to me over many years by my patients and people attending my seminars and lectures. I have mentioned the names of groups and courses only where I have heard similar and consistent stories from many separate sources.

There are at least a hundred known cults operating in Australia and it has been estimated that there are over one thousand operating in the United States. Personal development courses alone are currently attracting a turnover of one billion dollars annually in Australia. Nobody knows exactly what the financial turnover in cults is worth, as large-scale tax avoidance is common.

For this reason it should not be assumed that the groups, courses or individuals mentioned in this book are necessarily the worst or biggest. I have only mentioned those that are well known and where my own patients have shared their personal experiences with me.

Acknowledgements

This book could not have been written without the courage of all those people who have contacted me to disclose very personal information about themselves, their families and their experiences with cults, gurus and in personal development courses. The book is therefore a tribute to their courage, and to help them and their families further understand that they are not weak, gullible fools but victims of powerful techniques used without their consent.

And, as with my other books, this one could not have been written without the continued practical and emotional support of my husband John, who again typed the manuscript (this time on a new computer!), and my children, who took over much of the cooking and chores so I could work uninterrupted on the book.

Also, a big thank-you to my staff and close colleagues, who gave tremendous support as I coped with threats and intimidation by groups who hoped this book would never be published.

Introduction

Why is this book necessary?

One of my special interests as a psychologist is the use of techniques to control and heal the body – mindbody or 'ideodynamic healing'. This work means that the people who come to see me usually have chronic, long-standing or very serious physical conditions, that have been resistant to medical approaches. My patients have therefore almost all tried an enormous array of other health professionals, alternative treatments and 'courses' in frantic attempts to get well.

I have become increasingly alarmed, particularly over the last twelve months, at the number of people and their families in desperate need of help after attending personal development courses, leaving cults, or 'consulting' individuals such as faith healers, channellers and fortune tellers.

Since the publication of my last book, *Your Mindbody Energy*, which mentioned mind-control techniques, I have been overwhelmed by people wanting help and information about these techniques and how to recognise them. This need for consumer information grows ever greater and more urgent as we approach the year 2000, because many groups with quasi-religious or metaphysical beliefs are using the end of the millennium as a focus for their activities and recruitment.

In addition, the deep economic recession throughout the world has made nearly everyone uneasy about the future, leading to widespread insecurity and feelings of vulnerability. As I shall explain, such anxiety can put people in a state of heightened arousal, which in turn makes them more susceptible to the activities of individuals and groups wishing to manipulate people's beliefs about themselves, their families and society generally.

I have found the *consistency* of the stories most worrying: these have been recounted by highly credible people, detailing their experiences and claiming emotional and sexual abuse, blackmail, industrial espionage, manipulation, threats, suicide (which appeared to be triggered by experiences in cults and courses) and serious financial and tax frauds. These people were so frightened and intimidated that they would not 'go public' with their stories for fear of reprisal from the groups.

Those leaving cults whom I have spoken to often felt they had already lost everything – their families, friends, property, money – so that leaving in many ways could only be an improvement. But those involved in 'personal development groups', which may operate with the techniques of a cult but whose members remain at home and in their jobs, were struggling desperately to hang on to relationships, businesses and their emotional and physical health as they tried to leave the group's influence. It was these people who had most to lose by 'going public'.

Some brave souls have gone public with a good deal of

media coverage. This has resulted in greater public aware-ness of specific groups like Forum, Money and You, Kenja (a purely Australian cult), Scientology and Reiki. However, such discussion of individual groups, while extremely important, has not explained the *general psychological process being exploited by groups and the different kinds of techniques used by them on potential recruits.* Moreover, when exposed to widespread attention groups tend to just change their names and set up shop elsewhere.

Because the psychological techniques employed on potential members are so powerful there is no doubt that they can promote dramatic change. The problem is that when they are not used properly, and if the subjects are not screened adequately first, the outcome for the subjects can be extremely unpredictable – sometimes very good, some-times there is no apparent effect, but in many cases the results are devastatingly bad.

By detailing in this book the underlying psychological process that makes people vulnerable to recruitment by cults and similar organisations, its relationship to hypnosis, and the techniques used for 'persuasion', I hope to make it impossible for such groups to operate without their targets being immediately aware of the dangers involved.

ONE

The Techniques Groups Use

The terrifying events in Hitler's Germany and the development of the Cold War between America and Russia in the post-Second World War period led to an enormous interest in government organisations concerning the possibility that beliefs could be manipulated by either psychological or biochemical (drugs like LSD) methods.

The propaganda pictures shown on Russian television in the early 1950s, of American pilots shot down over Korea expounding the virtues of a communist society, sent shockwaves through the Western world. It resulted in a huge amount of research being undertaken, particularly in the USSR and America, into how such a thing could happen. This research was often covertly, but sometimes even overtly, financed by intelligence organisations and it became clear that two different phenomena were involved, 'brainwashing' and 'mind control'.

Brainwashing and mind control should not be confused. Brainwashing can occur when a person knows they are in a captive situation. It is commonly done by extreme physical and emotional abuse and can usually be quickly undone once the person is freed and no longer in danger. Mind

1

control is far more sophisticated. The victim does not see themselves as denied either physical or emotional freedom and there does not need to be any physical abuse for it to be successful. Without professional help mind control can be extremely difficult to undo, even when the person has left the group and wants to change.

At the same time as these mind-control and brainwashing techniques were being studied a new school of behavioural psychology was developing in America that was analysing animal and human behaviour and how it could be changed. This academic and clinical research was primarily aimed at developing therapeutic psychological techniques to help people, but as there were no restrictions on access to the information produced by researchers it quickly became available to others in the community, others *not* bound by any legal or ethical standards and who were accountable to no authority – legal or academic – regarding the way they used the techniques.

Significant numbers of cults using the new psychological techniques began to emerge in the early 1960s in America and then spread quite quickly to many different countries. The cults' employment of these procedures was known to authorities. Indeed, according to an ex-'Moonie', and since confirmed by other investigations, in America the CIA actively co-operated with the Moonies, encouraging the cult to use psychological techniques to 'process' and 'neutralise' student activists and leaders on university campuses protesting about America's involvement in the Vietnam War. In the decades since then, cults have grown both in numbers of active organisations and membership, and have continued to be very good at adapting new therapeutic psychological techniques for their own purposes.

Many of the cults which started in the 1960s continue to demand that their members live physically isolated from mainstream society. Such groups I call 'closed' cults and examples are the Children of God, Moonies and Orange People. However, as more sophisticated indoctrination techniques have been developed by cults it has become less necessary for them to impose physical isolation on recruits in order to control their behaviour. Thus over the last twenty years more and more groups have emerged who have all the characteristics of cults but are very open about their activities in the community. These I call 'open' cults, and include Hare Krishna (which was originally quite isolated) and Scientology.

Open cults have increasingly adopted socially acceptable guises in the community in order to be seen as less threatening to people. Hare Krishna, for instance, now run vegetarian restaurants. Other groups claim status as 'proper religions', such as the Moonies (whose official name is the Unification Church) and the Church of Scientology.

One of the easiest ways for open cults to gain access to vulnerable people in the community has been by setting up shop as psychotherapists (in many countries there are no restrictions on the use of this term) or by running 'personal growth' courses. These courses were originally aimed at individuals but are now being targeted increasingly at businesses.

Psychological techniques
Over the last ten years, and particularly during the past five years, there has been an absolute explosion of research by

clinical psychologists into new therapeutic techniques that are extraordinarily effective at helping people resolve past traumas, conflicts and personal relationship difficulties. Unfortunately, no restrictions on the use of these new techniques have come with these exciting developments. Neither has there been any legislation about who may use them. Many techniques have been further researched by sales and marketing organisations specifically to find ways of manipulating people into sales by changing their beliefs generally.

This misuse of therapeutic psychological practices is completely unknown to the public. However, many professionals are amazed and despairing at the lack of effective government regulation concerning the abuse of such powerful techniques. Government inactivity appears due to a variety of reasons. In part it is the result of a simplistic, ideological trend by present governments throughout the world to 'deregulate', regardless of the long-term effects on society. I suspect it is also due to the fact that some of these techniques are used widely by orthodox religions, so there is a misplaced reluctance by governments to try to clarify the often grey area between what is 'legitimate religion', and cultism and allied personal development groups. The issue is muddled further by some people saying that advertising is a form of mind control.

This fuzzy area of inadequate definition makes it easy for groups misusing psychological techniques to lobby against regulation, and resist any interference with what they do or how they live. The result in Australia has been that in 1982 Scientology was removed from control under the Psychological Practices Act in Victoria, while there have been difficulties for Community Services departments in Victoria and New South Wales in their legal proceedings against the Children of God sect to ensure proper care of the children in the cult. The recent tragedy in Waco, Texas, might have been averted had not government bodies shown extreme reluctance to intervene earlier. This appears to have been partly due to the difficulty of finding legitimate grounds for intervention that would have later stood up in court.

Any confusion between individual rights, acceptable group behaviour, legitimate religion and cults or gurus is a product of woolly thinking rather than a real problem of definition. *It should be clearly understood that while the general psychological process being used by orthodox religions or advertising to manipulate a person's beliefs and actions may be similar, even the same as, that used by cults, gurus and some personal development courses, the* accountability *of those using this process, and the question of whether those participating do so with* informed consent *(agreeing to participate only after knowing all the facts) makes the ethical position totally different.*

I think the issue of the accountability of orthodox religions, health professionals, advertising and the media could do with a thorough review, but at least it is accepted that they should be accountable to the community and the standards of their behaviour can be enforced. The organisations themselves recognise they should be accountable in such a way. The problem with cults, gurus, faith healers and many personal development groups is that in effect they are not accountable to anybody. Furthermore, they believe their activities should *not* be accountable to anyone!

The second fundamental difference between orthodox

groups and maverick ones is the informed consent of the participants. If you walk through the doors of any Christian church you know you are becoming involved in a particular belief system. If you go to a car yard you know you are going to be subjected to a polished sales technique trying to manipulate you into buying a car. Similarly, if you read an advertising brochure you *know* it is attempting to sell you something.

If you consult a health professional about a particular problem there is no doubt that you are seeking help to solve that problem, be it physical or emotional (although as a community we are demanding more and more that health professionals provide their patients with information about procedures so that they can give *informed consent* to treatment). However, none of the cults, gurus, group leaders or healers I have encountered, or those that people have complained to me about, have clearly stated what they are really selling – or described the powerful psychological techniques they intend to use – *before* the person is involved (and that means prior to 'information evenings'). People are therefore manipulated into participating *without* informed consent. Some organisations even seem to hide their aims: individuals have complained to me about a course called 'Money and You', which they thought was some sort of accountancy package – only to discover it was an intensive personal development course.

Educating the community

Our schools teach children a topic called Consumer Education, which is designed to alert them to their rights as consumers and the techniques they will be subjected to in order to get them to consume. Society recognises a need for such education and provides it as a balance to the interests of sellers, but people are not taught to recognise the disguised, psychological techniques employed by many personal development courses and cults.

Whenever I have asked people why they had not complained to Consumer Affairs about what had happened to them, they have all said that the group leaders had told them that their dissatisfaction was totally due to them being either 'not ready to benefit' or 'emotionally inadequate' people, and had nothing to do with the techniques – in other words, the blame was put on the victim. Because these distressed people did not recognise what had been done to them they were not able to take any action to combat it.

The leaders of groups using psychological techniques I have spoken to are not the slightest bit interested in any negative consequences of what they are doing. In fact, most have the attitude that if a few recruits are devastated and screwed up, it is justified by all the others that are being enlightened. (Unfortunately I once heard the same view expressed by a health professional, but regardless of a health professional's personal attitude he or she is still legally accountable to society and their patient has access to redress.)

Manipulating groups

While there is a general lack of awareness in the community about the misuse of psychological techniques, this is exacerbated by a similar lack of awareness amongst most psychologists and psychiatrists of the psychodynamics of very large groups. They do not know of the difference between techniques that can be used to manipulate large groups and those that are employed to achieve the same outcome with an individual. Psychologists and psychiatrists have intensive and long training in helping individuals. Sometimes (if they do extra training) they can help through working with small groups (about eight people). They have no training in working with groups of several hundred. The use of traditional hypnosis with individuals in therapy requires an extra two-year training course, so few psychologists and psychiatrists have a detailed knowledge of traditional hypnosis techniques.

Such ignorance of how hypnosis can be achieved in large meetings has resulted in a small number of health professionals attending sessions, succumbing to the group hypnosis and then themselves becoming involved in these groups. Such professionals have been quickly used by the organisations to give credibility to what they are doing.

In fact, it was not until I had observed meetings of these groups myself, spoken to many people who had been involved and done a great deal of reading from overseas that I became aware myself of the connection between what is done with individual patients in hypnosis and what was being attempted on a mass as well as individual scale by these cults, gurus, leaders and masters. *The psychological process employed by them was the same as hypnosis, although the techniques and methods used to gain psychological control of groups were not those traditionally associated with hypnotism.*

It also became apparent why people can be so easy to manipulate in these situations. If you tell somebody you are going to help them become hypnotised, then unless that person wants to be hypnotised it can be extremely difficult, if not impossible, to get them to enter a suggestible state. However, if you *don't* inform the person you are going to use hypnosis and then you create the right conditions, hypnotising a subject is *extremely* easy, while the person involved may be completely unaware of what is happening.

The effects of hypnosis done on large groups are enhanced by three extremely powerful social factors (called 'influence processes') which are also operating. These are: behaviour modification, obedience to authority and conformity to group expectations. They have been studied extensively since the Second World War to understand why ordinary people in the German and Japanese armies could carry out the appalling war crimes they did.

Behaviour modification techniques use positive or negative rewards to change people's behaviour without them being aware of it. A very well-known anecdote in psychology departments at universities is the story of a group of psychology students whose lecturer normally paced backwards and forwards in front of them while lecturing. The students smiled and looked interested whenever the lecturer moved to the left of the room and then frowned and looked bored and uninterested whenever he went to the right. Very soon the students had trained the lecturer to lecture from one spot only, but when confronted with what had been done he denied vehemently that his behaviour had in any way been influenced by the group and insisted that he was lecturing in a fixed position because he always did so!

Such behaviour modification is deliberately and widely used, albeit from the opposite standpoint, by leaders when they lecture to large groups to influence the group's behaviour and beliefs without them being in the least aware of what is happening.

The frightening power of how people will obey authority figures has also been studied extensively and was demonstrated most famously in the highly controversial experiments done by Stanley Milgram. Milgram found that over 90 per cent of people would obey orders to give people painful electric shocks if they felt the person giving the order appeared to have some kind of authority! This explains why it is so easy for groups to get people to lie, cheat, steal and even inflict physical violence: if they think they are carrying out the leader's wishes then they no longer regard themselves as responsible!

Other research has shown how people will go against their own beliefs about a situation and conform to whatever is being said or concluded by the most confident and self-assured people in the group – even if the group is quite small. Hence if people have doubts about what is being taught in cults or groups, or are not experiencing whatever 'wow' feeling that they are supposed to, they will suppress their doubts or blame themselves if the leader and others in the group insist what they are saying or doing is correct.

The power of the conformity influence process also makes it easier for group hypnosis techniques to be used as even when someone is instinctively reluctant to participate they will anyway – just to conform to and please the group.

What is hypnosis?
Hypnosis is not a state resembling sleep in any way. It is

not sleepwalking or sleeptalking, nor do you have to look at a swinging object or into someone's eyes in order to be hypnotised. It is a special, altered, state of mind, subjectively different from the natural alert state, where the subject's beliefs and perceptions about himself or herself and the world around them (even their most fundamental values) can be changed.

A person does not have to be particularly physically relaxed, nor have his or her eyes closed, in order to be in such a state. Furthermore, it is very easy to impart post-hypnotic suggestions so that the subject will not remember the details of what is happening under hypnosis *or listen to and process* any *criticism of the group, its activities or the leader.*

Suggestions that something terrible will happen to him, the world or his family if he leaves or criticises the group can also be implanted. These suggestions can be extremely powerful ways of controlling members (even if they do manage to leave), because the person can have post-hypnotic amnesia so that they have no conscious memory of the suggestions. Fears about the consequences of leaving the group can be developed to the point where they are real phobias, creating physical as well as emotional symptoms. Post-hypnotic suggestions can also be used by groups to get subjects to start active recruiting, so when they go home their friends and family can find they have become quite evangelical about their new beliefs. Post-hypnotic amnesia also explains why recruits can tell people how wonderful the new group is, but be completely unable to give coherent details about what happened.

It has been assumed by many traditional hypnotherapists

that you cannot get people to do something they do not really want to do by hypnotising them. This has been a comforting thought to clinicians, and may well be true if the person knows they are being hypnotised. But from my discussions with many patients involved in these groups, and my observations of their techniques, I do not believe this is true if a person is participating in hypnosis *without being aware of it.*

This is particularly true where confusional techniques are used. Confusional techniques give the person contradictory instructions, tasks to complete, or information that just doesn't make sense. The critical mind becomes so overwhelmed trying to evaluate what is being said or done that it just gives up trying.

Hypnosis has been used by man, especially in healing, for thousands of years. Traditional hypnotherapists tend to talk about hypnosis in terms of good and bad hypnotic subjects, the depth of the trance state and inducing hypnosis in a patient. However psychologists building on the recent work of Milton Erikson and Erni Rossi see hypnosis more as a natural healing state that utilises the connection between mind and body (this idea – that physical ailments can be changed by psychological means – is also called ideodynamic healing).

The natural healing state occurs in a cyclical way throughout the day and night, and can be accessed quite easily for effective hypnotherapy without the patient necessarily being in deep trance. These mindbody, or ideodynamic, techniques for healing and changing beliefs are far more subtle than traditional hypnosis, and are particularly relevant to understanding the techniques being used by cults, gurus and personal development courses and the psychological process they are exploiting.

If a psychologist is only trained in traditional hypnosis techniques he or she will probably miss the significance of many procedures used by cults. Ideodynamic techniques utilise a very sophisticated use of language, and cues from the patient's body language, to access quickly ways in which that person can be induced to change. Moreover, in traditional hypnosis relaxation is seen as very important to accessing the unconscious, but with ideodynamic techniques it has been discovered that an increased level of arousal can be equally important in allowing access to the unconscious mind.

TWO

Groups That Can Harm

~~~~~~

Cults, groups and individuals wanting to manipulate your beliefs or empty your wallet don't advertise their intentions, so they can be extremely difficult to recognise until you are already involved. Many groups regularly change their names or the locations they operate from once they are exposed or get any adverse media coverage. For this reason I do not attempt in this book to give a detailed analysis of every single cult, personal development course or guru causing problems, but rather to expose the general processes and techniques they use so that you can easily recognise attempts to manipulate your beliefs, regardless of the name used by those approaching you, or the circumstances.

It is often assumed that the main motivation of cults, gurus and personal development courses is money. While this is a crucial motivator, another motivation for leaders is the power they have over members of the group. This power can give leaders an extraordinary 'high'. In contrast, during the rigorous training of professionals there is particular focus on the problem of abuse of power in therapeutic relationships, including strong ethical and legal restraints on such abuses.

The financial and personal power of cult leaders and gurus is now being increasingly used to extend influence out of their immediate groups and into industry, business, politics and education. Many people who have contacted me have been involved in courses targeted at influential business and professional people. They expressed concern about the beliefs and values that were being pushed in these courses and the pressure to take these beliefs into their work places and communities.

As these groups become more sophisticated and have more members in prominent community positions they are becoming bolder in their approach. Transcendental Meditation, for instance, has already started a move into politics and is standing candidates at elections. There is nothing new in community groups lobbying government and gaining positions of influence or becoming active in politics, but cults disguised as community groups have hidden agendas.

The problem of interest groups having undue influence on government is an ongoing one in our society. I believe that political parties and politicians should be made to disclose the origin of all donations and support, and that this is crucial to maintain democracy, for otherwise politicians can feel beholden to generous donors. The rise in influence of pressure groups, their lobbying of politicians and per- suasion methods now being widely used make the need for public scrutiny of donations urgent.

A free society can support a myriad different views, values and cultures as long as all groups are equally accountable for their actions and can be equally scrutinised by the community as a whole. The danger and difference with many groups emerging now is that they don't consider themselves accountable in the same way that others do, nor do they allow themselves to be closely scrutinised by the community. Cults and personal development groups are not alone in this – unfortunately some sections of our judicial system also take this attitude about *their* accountability. If we allow this view to prevail we are setting a dangerous course!

CULTS

In cults there is a leader or guru. Guru is an Indian term that refers to a spiritual teacher or guide. In Indian culture gurus are highly respected holy men. However in the West the term is commonly used to refer to the leader of a cult or group that uses various eastern philosophies as part of its teachings.

The guru or leader (who may be living or dead) usually claims he or she is God or has been chosen by God to carry out some special purpose with a select few (the members of the cult). However, this purpose – and the beliefs of the cult – are generally not revealed until a person is well and truly involved with and dependent on the group.

Cults can be described as 'closed' or 'open'. In closed cults there is little contact between cult members and the wider community, and this is traditionally how society has believed cults operate. However, there are increasing numbers of cults that actively encourage members to operate normally in the community and to seek positions of power in the professions and public service. These open cults often have high profiles in the community and give the superficial appearance of being above board. Closed cults may dress in uniforms, such as the shaven heads and saffron robes of the Hare Krishna, while open cult members will be indistinguishable from the general public. Some cults that were once completely closed, like the Hare Krishna, are becoming quite open and adopting higher profiles in the general community, although members still tend to live in isolated communes.

With closed cults indoctrination into the cult usually starts with a simple invitation to meet some 'friends'. The location of the first meeting is often not the actual headquarters of the cult, but a less obvious and harmless-looking venue. From the moment someone is targeted by a cult member, systematic attempts to isolate the potential recruit begin. Once they are isolated strategies are operated to make them emotionally dependent on the group. These may take the form of stealing belongings (for instance, passport, handbag, money or wallet), giving them a special diet to eat that will affect their judgement, keeping them up all night talking, or making them take unusual and prolonged exercise. If a person targeted by a cult can be isolated from contact with friends or family, is without outside support and stays with the group for as little as forty-eight hours, there is a very high probability that he or she will become entangled long-term.

Once involved a cultist is very quickly separated emotionally and physically from his or her family and previous friends. The cult must become his or her whole life. In cults the leader or his deputy demands absolute obedience and the needs of the cult must always be put before those of the individual or the community at large. Often a cultist's life on earth is considered unimportant, and all emphasis is placed on the life after death – members of cults come to believe death will be the beginning of 'real' life.

Because of the techniques and rituals employed in cults' daily routines, cultists tend to be in alternate states of high arousal with hyper-vigilance, and very low arousal or trance-like states. This destroys their ability to think clearly and logically. In fact they may become easily disorientated and appear fidgety, fearful and highly suspicious of outsiders. Alternatively, especially as they rise in power within the cult, they may appear euphoric and 'not real' to outsiders.

Drugs are sometimes used to control members without their knowledge. The 'Hamilton-Byrne Family' cult at Eildon in Victoria, Australia, used LSD extensively on both children and adult members during the 1960s through their influence at a private psychiatric hospital. This cult deliberately targeted health professionals and some social workers so that it could 'legally' adopt over two hundred children. The children were isolated at the cult home in the country. The cult's influence within the Department of Education gained its 'private school' official recognition and it was subject to only minimal government supervision and interference. When locals' concern or complaints were received by Community Services, the cult's contacts within that department alerted it about raids being planned to investigate its activities. Consequently it took many years before the the cult was successfully exposed.

It is common for children in cults actively to be denied adequate education and thus prevented from obtaining skills that could make them independent of the cult. The children of a cult may not go to a normal community school but instead attend classes run by the cult itself which are not open to any kind of scrutiny by or accountability to education authorities.

Cults do not consider themselves answerable to the wider community. Their extreme isolation from the balancing values and perspective of outside society gives further power to the techniques they use.

Cultists often work extremely hard and for long hours at fundraising, manual work or worship. Tax evasion by cults and their members is common. Many kinds of cash busi- nesses tend to be operated, such as flower, chocolate and door-to-door selling, and market stalls. Some cults have at times actively encouraged prostitution, for instance the Children of God and, allegedly, the Sannyassin. It is both expected of members and a way of gaining approval from the group to give generously, not only financially but also of time. There are continual demands for members to prove 'commitment' in some way, for instance by donating money, recruiting others or attending courses.

Since the only measure and judgement of a cultist's degree of faith and commitment is the leader, cultists become extremely dependent on his approval. They must accept his teachings to gain recognition and approval from other cultists as well – for if someone is rejected or snubbed by the leader everybody else rejects them too.

The methods used by cults to control members can be quite subtle and sophisticated. Public humiliation of dissi- dents, or banishing them from contact with the leader for set lengths of time, can actually make people more depen- dent than ever on regaining the approval of the leader and the other followers.

Increasingly, open cults are attempting to blur their identity with personal development courses. A favoured approach by open cults is to offer 'psychotherapy' or personality testing. There are no regulations in many countries, including Australia, concerning who can call themselves a psychotherapist or practise psychotherapy*. Cults are increasingly incorporating technological hardware – computer questionnaires, tapes, 'psychological' tests (often of dubious reliability or scientific integrity) and electronic gadgetry – into their 'psychotherapy' sessions to make what they do seem more scientific and legitimate. These 'scientific' approaches appear to appeal particularly to men.

The Church of Scientology offers personality and IQ testing, psychotherapy and uses an 'E-Meter' to help reveal emotional issues that they feel a person should be addressing. Scientologists call this 'auditing'.

The E-Meter appears to be a type of biofeedback machine. It apparently measures the electrical conductivity of the skin (the Galvanic Skin Response or GSR). People tend to sweat

---

* **Psychiatrists, psychologists and psychotherapists**

A *psychiatrist* is a medical doctor who has specialised in the treatment of people who are mentally ill or who have behavioural or emotional problems. Psychiatrists use drugs, electroconvulsive therapy (ECT) and psychotherapy to treat patients. They may see patients for just a few sessions or many times a week for many months or even years. Some psychiatrists are now using a number of therapies created and used by psychologists.

There are many different types of *psychologists*: clinical, counselling, neuropsychological, organisational, sports, educational. In this book the term 'psychologist' is used to denote a psychologist who treats people who have behavioural, relationship or emotional problems (clinical and counselling psychology). Such psychologists have 8–12 years of training, which is a combination of academic courses at university and clinical training with patients. Psychologists do not use

more when there is an increase in their level of arousal and this causes an increase in the level of electrical conductivity of the skin. Operators of these meters (which are very like crude lie-detector machines) assume that if the GSR increases while they are talking to a subject or asking questions it indicates they have triggered some emotional problem that needs fixing. *This can be an extremely misleading and inaccurate assumption.* What the E-meter is measuring – apart from the ability of the auditor to upset the subject – is highly dubious, but the use of a machine to check your emotional health can be extremely attractive because it seems so simple and scientific. (See also the section on the Church of Scientology on pages 29–34.)

Because of the intimate information cults using these such techniques gather about their members and encourage them to reveal – during 'auditing', 'psychotherapy' or similar sessions – the members tend to become highly vulnerable to the group and dependent on keeping its approval.

drugs or ECT. Instead they use a variety of therapies – cognitive behavioural, family, EMDR (Eye Movement Desensitisation and Reprogramming) – designed to change or modify patients' behaviour, beliefs and attitudes and resolve past traumas. Psychologists tend to see patients over short periods of time, on average 6–12 sessions.

The term *psychotherapy* was originally applied to psychoanalysis as described by Sigmund Freud and used mainly by psychiatrists. Recently it has come to mean the use of any 'therapy' to address psychological/emotional/behavioural/ relationship problems. Because there are no restrictions on who can call themselves a 'psychotherapist' the term is increasingly being used by anybody untrained who wishes to give themselves an official-sounding title. In this book the term 'psychotherapy' is used in its modern, widespread sense.

Open cults are extremely polished at managing the media. They arrange friendly interviews and have supportive letters written to the editors of newspapers and magazines. Members have suggested to me that cults are using the law to protect themselves – for instance, some claim to have no funds for a legal defence answering charges being made against them, while others may mount vexatious libel suits to prevent any criticism, however well-founded, being published.

Cults often go to extreme lengths to protect themselves from criticism. Apart from vexatious libel suits some have threatened and even physically assaulted anyone who criticises them. Some cults have specific organisations set up to mount campaigns to discredit critics, to the extent of framing critics for criminal offences or telling deliberate lies about their personal lives.

Open and closed cults thrive on the tendency of the community not to want to interfere in areas traditionally viewed as private, family responsibilities. Child abuse and violence in our society are easy to get away with while we are so reluctant to take on the welfare of vulnerable individuals as a collective community responsibility rather than something 'private'. We should not be hesitant when it comes to making a stand on community expectations of how children are reared. It is *not* an infringement of civil liberties or religious freedom to make everyone accountable for how they treat children, nor to say that emotional and physical violence in relationships is *not* acceptable regardless of the beliefs held by the participants. Physical and emotional abuse of adults is extremely common in cults, while children are even more at risk: many cults use puberty as the age children are forced to begin sexual relations, with the leader or someone else of his choice.

It is *vital* to have general community standards against which behaviour and beliefs can be measured, for otherwise cults are allowed to go unchallenged. The bottom line is that if cults have nothing to hide why do they insist on being exempt from accountability to the wider community?

While most cults use very similar techniques to convert people to their particular belief systems, and to maintain compliance thereafter, they vary enormously in the beliefs they hold, the numbers of members involved, their specific values and how they live.

Cults may be extremely small and live as a single 'family' unit. Neighbours may not even realise the people next door are a cult. The size of a cult tends to grow over time as the leader becomes more and more obsessed by his own power, until they may have thousands of members and a high public profile in many countries, for instance Hare Krishna, the Unification Church (usually known as the Moonies), and the Children of God. Cult members may live communally, or independently, or a mixture of both.

Many cults use traditional eastern and Christian religions as a basis for their beliefs, to make it easier to gain acceptance as true 'religions'. Official religious status gives cults tax advantages, and also gives them increased acceptance in the community. Other cults discard established religions and have their own set of rules completely, based on the teachings of the leader.

There are thousands of cults in existence; many are known

only to their own members but some have become notorious. The following descriptions of six well-known cults should provide a better understanding of their similarities and the breadth of their differences. They also demonstrate the effects that a cult has on the leader himself. Some of the most dangerous cults have been started by people who have become aware of having a natural ability to lead. Without exception the power the leaders experience over others, together with the money members provide, destroys any initial positive aspirations. The leaders lose touch with reality – and acceptable standards of behaviour – and exploitation of the members becomes endemic.

The People's Temple

The extraordinary potential power of cults was dramatically brought home to the world in 1978 when more than nine hundred members of Jim Jones's People's Temple committed mass suicide by poison on his instructions at the cult's headquarters, Jonestown in Guyana, South America.

Jim Jones originally trained as a Disciples for Christ minister, but later left to start his own sect in Northern California. Like many leaders he attracted followers with his vision for a better social system. He initially recruited from poor and lonely people but soon realised that this group did not have the financial resources to further his dreams.

He then started recruiting middle-class, well-educated and financially secure people in their twenties and thirties (although later his members came from all age groups). He quickly learned ways of making money fast – by taking a proportion of the pay cheques of his followers, by fostering children and receiving social security payments for their care, and by direct 'witnessing' (door-knocking for donations). Subsequently members had to prove their commitment by signing over their assets, and gained recognition by manipulating their families who were not in the cult.

To show their faith followers confessed in sworn affidavits to having committed crimes or sexual perversions. Jones used these as blackmail on members who tried to leave or questioned his authority. Jones would also make parents sign guardianship of their children over to him and used his treatment of the children as a weapon against the parents.

He deliberately became politically active in order to receive favours from government, and friendly mentions in the local press. Initially this was done by providing numerous unpaid campaign workers to do menial but essential tasks in political campaigning for candidates. Later he became active in the local judiciary system (Foreman of the Mendocino County grand jury) and even held a seat on the county Juvenile Justice and Delinquency Prevention Board.

He had a highly effective publicity machine that made sure photographs of him with famous people like Jane Fonda, Walter Mondale and Hubert Humphrey were widely circulated. His community and charity work with the poor was always well publicised.

Increasingly he used drugs, both himself and on his followers. His sexual perversions and abuse of children and adults were the reason many investigations were started into his activities. In order to quell any criticism Jones had a Diversions Unit, whose job was to start spreading damaging rumours about anyone who was publicly criticising him. The media and authorities investigating the cult often fell for this ploy, becoming so tied up with examining the credibility of the person complaining that Jones's activities were largely ignored.

Jones encouraged followers to prove their commitment and gain favours by reporting on their friends, spouses or other cult members who had breached rules. (Cults often have large numbers of rules, so there can be plenty of opportunity to punish members who break them inadvertently.) The fact that nobody could trust anybody else increased their dependency on Jones. As Jones became more and more involved with using drugs his paranoia about 'the outside' increased and finally he left for Guyana to create his settlement, Jonestown, from the slave labour of his followers and their children.

Many of the children he took to Guyana were removed from their parents using the guardianships he had acquired. It was an international custody battle between the parents of one such child – who had themselves left the cult – that triggered the mass suicide at Jonestown.

Initially Jones had seen himself as the inheritor of the spirits of Jesus, Buddha and God, but later on he believed and preached that he was actually God.

The Children of God

This cult was started in the early 1970s in America by a dismissed Baptist minister, David Berg. He began his career as an assistant to a television evangelist and soon set up a group called 'Teens for Christ'. This was later changed to 'Revolutionaries for Christ' and then 'Children of God'. More recently it became known as 'The Family'. With increasing bad publicity, there have been further name changes and a splitting of the main cult into many affiliated groups, based in Europe, Korea, Japan, Australia and New Zealand as well as America.

In the early 1970s Berg attracted a large number of young men because he could ordain them as ministers and they could thus avoid the Vietnam War draft. He also used his contacts with television evangelists to recruit members and solicit money on air. The cult and its financial resources grew extremely quickly.

Soon Berg abandoned the Bible to create his own religion, and changed his name to Moses Berg. His teachings to his followers became known as the 'Mo letters'. His members spent all their time aggressively recruiting young, isolated or disillusioned people on the streets, at airports and bus stations, and collecting money. As proof of commitment to Mo (and to be accepted into the Children of God, who were to be the chosen few to survive the 'ending of the world' as predicted by Mo to be going to occur first in 1986 and then in 1993) recruits signed over all their possessions to him. While Mo and his inner circle lived in luxury all the followers experienced extreme poverty.

Mo's teachings soon actively promoted prostitution and sex in order to recruit members – the cult called this 'Hookers for Christ'. Sexual abuse of children and other members was commonplace and considered acceptable practice, as was incest and sexual relationships with many partners.

When investigations into the cult's activities increased Berg became quite paranoid towards the outside world. His teachings encouraged his followers to isolate themselves more and more from the wider community. Children were provided with 'flee bags' that held a few essential items, to be ready at all times in case they needed to disappear at a moment's notice from authorities investigating the cult's activities. To avoid the scrutiny of authorities the cult splintered into smaller groups all over the world, but there is frequent travelling by members, particularly children, between countries.

As a smokescreen to counter authorities' reaction to the 'Mo letters' alternative, more acceptable teachings have been printed for public show. However, people who have recently left the cult in Australia have told me that the Children of God still basically follow Mo's original teachings – although they no longer use sex for recruitment purposes because of the danger of AIDS.

In 1992 the Community Services departments in New South Wales and Victoria raided two Children of God homes and took custody of the children. The children have since been returned to their 'families' under supervision orders but the case in Victoria is still legally unresolved as the Children of God claim they do not have the money to defend themselves in court and therefore it has been ruled that proceedings be adjourned indefinitely. (The Children of God initially applied for and received legal aid but because the legal aid system was in financial difficulties and the case promised to become extraordinarily expensive, their later application for further support was refused.)

At first the cult effectively used the media to attack the actions of the authorities and the social workers in removing the children. Such a diversionary tactic has been used repeatedly by cults all over the world.

This cult has allegedly been particularly effective at avoiding the law regarding children's attendance at properly recognised schools. Consequently as the cult's children grow up they will be socially, emotionally and educationally poorly equipped to cope with normal society. This means that as teenagers and adults they will be extremely dependent on the cult and unlikely to be able to leave successfully as they just will not have any skills necessary to live independently.

Former members have told me that in recent times the most prevalent and more insidious form of child abuse has been emotional rather than sexual or physical. Although 'spanking' regularly occurs for misdemeanours, it is also used if a child displays normal emotional responses such as anger, frustration or crying. Children are indoctrinated with an extreme fear of outsiders and of society in general, which is seen as the enemy of the cult.

The Church of Scientology

L. Ron Hubbard, a science fiction writer, founded Scientology (but not as a church) in 1951 after he published a book called *Dianetics: The Modern Science of Mental Health*. Hubbard believed everybody carries around emotional scars, called 'engrams', resulting either from his or her present life or a previous one.

According to Hubbard, people need to 'process' these engrams in 'auditing sessions' with a Scientologist counsellor in order to reach their full potential and be happy. The counsellor uses an E-meter (as described previously). This was patented by Hubbard and is basically like a very primitive biofeedback machine or lie detector. Using it the 'auditor' claims to discover and interpret 'engrams', or areas of emotional conflict, as he questions the subject.

In the early 1950s the use of hypnosis by psychiatrists and psychologists in therapy was mainly restricted to approaches requiring decreased arousal: relaxation and trance states. Hence Hubbard claimed what he was doing was not hypnosis, as it was having the opposite effect: 'waking people up'. What he didn't realise (and apparently his followers still don't) is that the process of hypnosis, dampening down critical left-brain thinking in order to access beliefs, unconscious processes and experiences through the right brain, can be even more effective when arousal is *increased*.

The Scientologists freely admit that the aim of their E-meter (which they claim is not based on the galvanic skin responses even though they agree it won't work if a person is cold or their hands are callused and dry) is to explore areas of a person's experience that will *increase arousal*. They then question the person while he or she is in this highly aroused state in order to change their behaviour and beliefs by 'clearing' them of reactions to past experiences and traumas.

Hubbard believed, and Scientology literature states: '. . . other practices such as hypnotism consider that a person has to be put into a state of lessened awareness i.e. a trance before anything can be done. Auditing is quite the opposite and seeks to wake people up'. But as I explain in this book, increased arousal states can be used to manipulate beliefs just as effectively as decreased arousal.

Questions like, 'Is this related to your relationship with your mother?' put to a person who is in a highly aroused state (for instance, contemplating their lack of confidence) can have the effect, when their ability to critically evaluate the question or situation is impaired, of making them assume that the problem *is due* to their mother.

Scientologists pride themselves that in auditing sessions the auditor *accepts everything* the person says. This can be highly dangerous as it is well established that the conclusions and information a person provides in circumstances of high arousal or very low arousal can be totally inaccurate or distorted perceptions of what actually happened. If this information is blindly accepted then the person himself accepts it as true, which can have disastrous consequences for long-standing relationships. Childhood resentments can be magnified, so a memory of being smacked by a father can be interpreted as the father being a sadist. Just because the father, like many parents, has smacked the child for misdemeanours does not make him a sadist. But a conclusion like this, uncritically accepted, can come to be believed as fact.

Even more worrying is the intensity of these sessions. During the weeks of an auditing course, the participant is expressly forbidden from discussing what is occurring with anyone (particularly family and friends) other than his particular auditor. It is common for initial auditing to be done as two-and-a-half-hour sessions *daily*. This usually adds up to seventy-five hours over a six-week period! That is a daily session in a highly aroused state where the participant is at the mercy of the auditor's questions, and isolated over that time from any balancing opinions. This number and frequency of sessions is considered by Scientologists to be the *minimum* needed.

The sessions are made even more powerful by the fact that they are of two and a half hours' duration, which means in every session a person is also going into a period of natural hypnosis associated with the body's ultradian rhythm. Furthermore, the Scientologists claim that their 'auditing' 'works one hundred percent of the time when it is properly applied to a person who sincerely desires improvement in his life'. This is a useful argument that if it's not working for you and making you miserable, it's because you are not sincere enough – not because there is something wrong with the technique.

Scientologists also call people who do not succumb to auditing 'anti-social personalities' or a 'potential trouble source', because they undermine the belief that Scientology always works and can do no harm. They have specific techniques to deal with such trouble sources. If necessary they will be expelled from the Church.

According to their literature, other 'impediments to receiving benefits' from auditing are 'receiving training while connected with someone who is against spiritual betterment', for instance, the family, 'discussing one's case with anyone other than their "auditor" or "examiner" [the auditor's supervisor]' or 'not getting auditing often enough'.

Auditing sessions are very expensive and people have paid up to tens of thousands of dollars for repeated auditings and other courses which the organisation offers. The basic belief that you have to be audited means that all members immediately have to pay the organisation significant sums of money, while at the same time revealing information and thus making themselves vulnerable to the cult. There have been many charges and claims by ex-members that information gained during auditing sessions (which may be taped) is then used against members if they try to leave the 'church'. Scientology began calling itself a church a few years after it started, which has provided it with tax advantages and better community acceptance. Even though the Church of Scientology has now gained legal acceptance in many countries as a 'church' it should be remembered that this does not mean that it cannot also be a cult. In fact the dictionary definition of a cult is 'a particular kind of religious worship'.

Scientology actively involves itself in the community and encourages members to gain positions of influence. It is now a huge and extremely wealthy empire, with branches world-wide. In Victoria, Australia, the Church of Scientology was banned between 1966 and 1982 because of its activities. Somehow, it successfully lobbied to have the ban repealed and the 'church' now operates and flourishes in the centre of Melbourne, along with every other Australian state capital city. This is despite the 1965 report of a Board of Inquiry set up by the Victorian government, generally known as the Anderson Report, which stated:

Scientology is evil; its techniques evil . . . Scientology is a grave threat to family and home life. As well as causing financial hardship, it engenders dissension, suspicion and mistrust amongst members of the family. Scientology has caused many family estrangements. The Board has been unable to find any worthwhile redeeming feature in Scientology . . .

Scientology is a delusional belief system, based on fiction and fallacies and propagated by falsehood and deception . . . It involves the administration by persons without any training in medicine or psychology of quasi-psychological treatment, which is harmful medically, morally and socially.

In the United States there have been many investigations into the cult, with claims of threats, blackmail, kidnapping and physical violence being made against those who oppose it. The Church asserts the stories are nonsense, but the findings of the American investigations and subsequent convictions of some Church leaders, including Hubbard's wife, appear quite conclusive in supporting these allegations.

In the last few months I have listened to alarming stories from distraught and miserable ex-members of this 'church'. The numerous courses and auditing sessions these people had paid to attend appeared to have dramatically undermined, and possibly destroyed, their relationships with their families. They also gave consistent descriptions of being harassed when they tried to leave.

Hare Krishna

The 'Krishna' religion is an Indian religion dating back to the late 1400s that grew out of traditional Hinduism. The Hare Krishna cult worship many gods, and love for the gods is demonstrated by long periods of repetitive dancing, singing and chanting. It was brought to the West by Swami Prabhupada in 1966. First based in New York, it grew rapidly.

The cult is extremely wealthy and runs many legitimate businesses, such as a number of vegetarian restaurants, farms and an incense business. The cult members live a communal life, with men and women segregated. The diet regime is strict, and many religious rituals are performed throughout the day.

This group has modified its extremely aggressive recruiting methods over the years and now blurs the distinction between religion and cult better than most. My concern about it – as with many of these groups – is that people become involved by being subjected to highly sophisticated psychological techniques without being able to give informed consent.

Women are considered inferior to men in Hare Krishna and the birth of a girl can be seen as divine punishment if permission for conceiving a child had not been first obtained from the Swami. Because girls are considered inferior they are not given an equivalent education to boys. I regard any group preaching beliefs that women are inferior and then attempting to influence society with its attitudes as absolutely abhorrent. Such views are totally inconsistent with the inherent values of our community and its laws.

The Unification Church (The Moonies)

Sun Myang Moon started his group in Korea in the mid-1940s. However, the Unification Church as such was not founded until 1951. The goal of this cult is that all religions in the world should be combined into one, which will then 'rule' the world. Sun Myang Moon declares that politics and church should not be separated and his cult is probably the most guardedly open cult in its intentions of gaining power through active political involvement.

Moon believes that Jesus' 'mistake' was not to be politically active. He does not intend to make the same error.

Moon also preaches that Jesus was supposed to marry and create a perfect family, but unfortunately he was killed first, so it is now his job to create this family – resulting in the huge marriage ceremonies he conducts with thousands of couples at once. The participants are chosen by him and may not have met their partners until just before the ceremony.

The Moonies have achieved extraordinary wealth (it is estimated their assets run into hundreds of millions of dollars). Their extremely aggressive and sneaky recruitment methods – and extensive use of the psychological techniques described in detail in Chapter 3 – have resulted in a virtual army of slave labour working for the cause, mainly in the United States, Japan and Korea. It has been estimated that there are in excess of three million Moonies worldwide. There has been growing alarm in the United States over this group's activities and its suspected political influence – especially when Moon managed to attend President Reagan's swearing-in ceremony seated in a section reserved for guests of the president.

As mentioned earlier, a number of ex-Moonies have claimed that the cult had a co-operative association with the CIA during the Vietnam War and it has been alleged that Moon has successfully promoted the interests of the South Korean government to US administrations. As the US tax and immigration departments have become increasingly interested in Moon's affairs he has moved most of his activities to Japan and Korea. However there are still Moonie businesses and followers throughout America.

It was the heartbreaking story told by a mother who came to see me many years ago, about what had happened to her children in the Moonies, that first triggered my interest in such groups. This woman's three daughters and a son, all teenagers, had travelled to the United States on their own to visit relatives they had never seen. It had taken the family years to save the money for the fares from a very modest income and the children's holiday jobs. The children were to connect with another flight at Los Angeles for the eastern states of America, but an industrial dispute left them in limbo at Los Angeles airport.

The children became panic-stricken when they discovered the bag the eldest was carrying with all their money and passports had been stolen. They were befriended by 'two lovely young people' who offered to help, and since the flight was delayed indefinitely they accepted the offer of accommodation for the night.

All four then disappeared. When distraught parents and relatives tried to find them the airport police immediately suspected they had been taken by the Moonies. Some months later the son turned up – sick, exhausted and suffering from severe malnutrition – and confirmed this. The parents managed to discover that all three girls had been ordered to marry and sent out of America.

The family have never heard from the three girls again. It has now been over twenty years since they disappeared. I have since heard from a number of other families who have lost *all* their children to the Moonie cult in very similar circumstances.

The Rajneesh Movement (Orange People)

The leader of this cult, Bhagwan Shree Rajneesh, was born in India where as a young man he started the 'Rajneesh

Movement', which is based on a mixture of eastern religions and philosophies. In the early 1970s Rajneesh already had a following of about 500 000 people. He travelled widely promoting his answers to the world's problems and found a ready source of recruits among the disillusioned hippies of the West. At one time Rajneesh instructed his followers to wear orange – hence their name – but this was later changed. Orange People now wear ordinary clothes in order to pass without comment in society.

Although Rajneesh centres flourished around the world in the 1970s and 1980s the cult became centred in Oregon, America, until charges of attempted murder, racketeering, fraud, conspiracy, immigration violation and electronic eavesdropping were made in 1984 against Rajneesh, his secretary Sheila, and a number of his administrators. Rajneesh left for India after receiving a suspended sentence, but Sheila is still serving a twenty-year jail term in the United States.

The cult moved back to India with Rajneesh. After the bad publicity surrounding the trials and Rajneesh's later death the branches of the cult in other countries have gone more underground but still definitely exist. Some ex-Orange People have now started up their own cults.

In Australia the main centre is at Yarra Glen in Victoria. It is run by a woman called Rachana and her husband, Derricha. According to investigation by journalists, which ties in with various accounts related to me by people who have been associated with the cult, the Australian branch first called themselves 'The Institute for Postural Integration'. The cult then changed its name several times in the last few years, and its names include 'Australia's New Age University',

'The Institute for Holistic Integration' and now 'Sannyassin'.

The techniques used by them for recruitment and indoctrination cover almost the full range described in this book. Women have apparently been encouraged to prostitute themselves to pay for 'courses' in personal development and healing. The Australian Orange People also run childbirth education classes and encourage home deliveries of babies at their commune. It is common for people to be introduced to this cult through one of the many courses they run, both at the commune itself and in the Melbourne suburbs. The topics covered at introductory lectures can be as diverse as childbirth education and UFOs.

PERSONAL DEVELOPMENT COURSES

Personal development courses can be run for a few hours, a day, over a few days or at regular times over many weeks. They can be residential, either for short or long periods of time. They offer almost anything that may improve your life: better, more natural childbirth; learning massage; improving self awareness; emotional 'growth'; physical healing; accessing psychic powers and 'cosmic consciousness'; better relationships; conflict resolution; making money; effective parenting; influencing people; sales techniques; self-discovery; metaphysics; the secrets of UFOs . . .

I wish to make it clear that as a psychologist I feel that personal development courses, when properly run by appropriately qualified, accountable professionals, can be an extremely safe and effective way of helping people to gain skills quickly or to change their attitudes in order to improve their quality of life, physical or emotional health as well as their relationships. For instance, the STEP program for improving parenting skills can be effective and valuable if run by a properly qualified teacher.

Many people who attend a personal development group say it was a wonderful experience that changed their lives for the better; others say it had no real effect except to empty their wallet. I fully accept that the psychological techniques they use are so powerful they can cause dramatic shifts in beliefs and attitudes within hours, and that *sometimes* this can be an improvement for the participants. My concerns are that people attending maverick courses are not adequately screened before attending, do not participate with informed consent about the possible dangers, the group or leader has no accountability for their actions and leaders are inappropriately or inadequately trained for what they are doing. This makes the outcome for the participants totally unpredictable, and puts them at great risk. It is not acceptable to say the risk of damage to some people is justified by the dubious possibility of benefits to others.

There are much safer, kinder and more respectful ways of helping people change and reassess their beliefs, values and priorities than implanting ideas from an external source while deliberately inhibiting their ability to think clearly and critically.

The personal development courses I consider dangerous are groups run by organisations or individuals who have either non-existent or inappropriate qualifications for what they are doing, and effectively are accountable to no one. The courses I worry about particularly are those attempting dramatic changes in short periods of time, such as Landmark

Education, EST, Forum, Money and You and Hoffman Process, for they are misusing the psychological techniques allied to hypnosis in order to make the behavioural changes.

At present in Australia there is an epidemic of personal development courses led by unqualified people. In every one I have observed or have been told about there has been consistent misuse of hypnosis – sometimes by people who had no idea what they were doing was in fact hypnosis. More worrying still is the number of groups using regression hypnosis techniques, which even fully trained professionals are extremely cautious about employing. The misuse of regressional hypnosis is particularly apparent in 'rebirthing'.

Regressional hypnosis is a technique by which a person can be taken back in time to various ages, in order to recall events that consciously may have been either partially or fully repressed. These are generally extremely unhappy experiences, such as sexual abuse in childhood or veterans' war experiences. Regressional hypnosis is only used therapeutically by psychiatrists or psychologists under strict safeguards and with extreme caution. *It is not necessarily beneficial for someone to remember very traumatic events consciously, and doing so in fact can cause them to become quite psychotic.* During rebirthing (also known as 'breath of life'), people with no formal training in psychology act as 'rebirthers'; they use breathing techniques to induce trance-like states in their subjects and expose emotional issues and memories they claim are blocking the subjects' full potential.

During rebirthing sessions there is often a great deal of anguished crying, screaming, pounding of pillows or self to 'release the blocks'. People with asthma can be at particular risk with rebirthing as they can develop powerful delusions that they do not need medication even as they turn blue from lack of oxygen!

Increasingly personal development courses are being subsidised indirectly by governments through allowing community houses and schools to be used as venues. The co-ordinators of these facilities are often not in a position to vet the people offering courses adequately, especially as many untrained course 'facilitators' are excellent con men and women. Teachers of such courses are often called 'leaders', 'trainers' or 'facilitators'.

A person with excellent training as a yoga teacher would be an ideal choice for leading a yoga course. However many people are now dabbling in areas they don't fully understand. They are running courses involving psychological techniques without any appropriate background or training. The first rule in running any personal development course should be for the leader to know their limitations and do no harm. Just because someone appears to be the kindest, most caring, loveliest person you – the potential customer – have ever met does not mean he or she can do no harm. Sadly, such people can and they do.

I am seeing more and more people who have attended personal development courses run by naturopaths, yoga teachers, meditation teachers, GPs, dentists and physiotherapists, as well as people calling themselves masters or gurus. The attendees are in serious psychological crises directly due to the ignorant abuse of extremely powerful psychological techniques. Just as I am not appropriately qualified to run an aerobics class, an ex-PE teacher or a physiotherapist is not qualified to run a psychotherapy group.

We are also seeing 'flying squads' of trainers arriving from overseas, doing their 'shows' and disappearing again. They do not have to register with anyone, or gain any official approval for what they are doing. They cannot be held accountable for the devastation they may leave behind. Money and You is one personal development course that uses imported trainers.

Many personal development courses are not open about their operations or goals until people actually attend. A number of people I have spoken to had attended Money and You, a course organised in Australia by an accounting firm. They thought they were there to learn how to manage their money, start a business and become millionaires. Instead they became involved in an extremely intensive personal development course that preached an unrealistic black-and-white view of human potential – essentially that they could become anything they wanted to, provided they were motivated enough with the right attitudes and 'discarded' anything that was holding them back, for instance their families!

Money and You is also involved in running residential groups for teenagers. I was told by their agent in Australia that even though the kids were put through an extremely intensive group-therapy-type residential workshop the trainers were all 'salesmen and marketing experts' from America. What damage will they be doing to those children's minds?

There are a number of groups now approaching companies in business and industry to run personal development courses as motivators for executives. If I were an employer there is no way I would allow my staff, who have confidential company and product knowledge, to attend. Many people who contacted me were very worried about the information they had found themselves divulging in the groups – and the confidential information they had learned about other companies' activities. Divulging secrets is a recognised method of gaining power over people (see Chapter 4), and is therefore a common technique used in personal development courses.

INDIVIDUALS

Call them what you will, gurus, masters, leaders or faith healers may operate on their own or with the backing of small or extremely large international organisations – generally cults. The guru business is now a booming industry worth billions of dollars a year.

The one thing that stands out with all gurus and leaders is how much they love the job! Very ordinary people can gain exceptional incomes, recognition and power in these roles. For people whose life may be fairly bland and seem insignificant the role of guru can give them an extraordinary emotional high, a reason for being, an income and power over others all at once. Frequently leaders come to believe their own publicity – that they have some divine mission in life or gift of healing.

For the followers, the feeling that they are one of a group that has been 'chosen' for some special mission immediately makes their ordinary human lives more important and special. This need to feel valued, special and recognised acts as a powerful motivator and is easily exploited by the leader. Approval of the member and personal recognition by the leader, and consequently the group, becomes an extremely powerful reinforcement to ensure compliant behaviour. As a person becomes increasingly dependent on and addicted to this approval his or her behaviour can become more and more at odds with their old beliefs and values. If the leader's approval is withdrawn then the follower can suffer physical and emotional feelings similar to those experienced by addicts withdrawing from drugs.

Many leaders I have observed and spoken to have studied neuro-linguistic programming techniques extensively so that they can use minute body cues (like eye movements) to 'read the patient'. They can then reprogram the 'patient's' (recruit's) values and beliefs just by the way they use language (see Chapter 3).

In therapy that will be beneficial to the patient the needs of the therapist must never override or interfere with the needs of the patient. However gurus or masters always put their needs above those of the followers, although this can be well camouflaged.

If a leader feels a need to wear special or unusual clothes, continually reminding others verbally or non-verbally how much they have suffered and survived, then they may well be using their illness and suffering to give them a special identity, fulfil their own needs and play a role. This makes the observer feel sympathy for them, and inhibits any tendency to criticise what they are doing – even when serious doubts arise.

People who have recovered from life-threatening illnesses often feel they have a mission to spread beliefs about their healing. Their intentions may be good, but having survived cancer does not give training in ideodynamic healing using complex psychological techniques. Ian Gawler is one of a number of leaders who have experienced miraculous cures, but he is trained as a vet!

People attending healing courses have told me that they have felt real concern about activities they were witnessing, but because the leader had been at some time very sick him/herself they felt extremely reluctant to criticise. Just because a person has been ill *does not* absolve them of their responsibility to others, nor does it necessarily give them special 'powers' to help. Having been seriously ill does not mean the leader can do no wrong – whether deliberately or unconsciously. This is particularly so when psychological techniques are being used in combination with extreme dietary regimes, fasting, enemas and megadoses of vitamins and minerals.

Healers

Apart from leaders running healing sessions akin to personal development courses, faith healers and 'reiki' also offer healing to the seriously ill. There are also individuals who simply decide to call themselves healers.

Faith healers use a fascinating array of tricks, gadgetry and showmanship to 'heal'. What they are probably doing is stimulating the body's own healing response with a placebo effect. Unfortunately they may be charging thousands of dollars to do it!

'Reiki' is a Japanese term meaning 'life energy'. It is a very simple technique that has been used by many cultures like the Australian Aborigines for tens of thousands of years. This simple technique has now been turned into an enormous multi-national, multi-level marketing business, operating mainly in Germany, Japan, America, Australia and New Zealand.

In order to sell such a basic phenomenon – accessing the body's electromagnetic field for ideodynamic healing, or emotional and spiritual renewal – which really only takes a few minutes to learn, reiki has been surrounded by two to three days or nights of group activities, including hypnosis. Reiki uses many of the techniques used by cults like the Moonies and the Orange People to convince attendees that they have been tuned-in to a secret, powerful energy. The next step is to learn to use it for healing other people – at a cost, of course. Students can go on to do courses at different levels.

There are actually three different businesses competing with each other although each claim to be the only one 'true' reiki. Two of them believe you must pay to attend seven different levels to become a 'Grand Master' (someone who can 'tune-in' other people). The third group only has a three-tiered marketing set-up. It costs about $200 to complete Level 1, about $500 to complete Level 2 and about $10 000 to become a Grand Master through the three-tiered organisation!

Or you can read my last book, *Your Mindbody Energy*, and teach yourself for nothing!

The seven-level course is more profitable for the organisers, costing about $20 000 to become a Grand Master. A Master who wanted one of my patients to pay to become a Master too assured him that he could earn at least $100 000 on a $10 000 investment in the first twelve months alone! But as more and more people pay their money to be tuned-in there is now a glut of Grand Masters coming on to the market and I believe that the price has recently started to come down.

Basically with reiki you pay to be convinced that you now have a special power when in fact you had it all along! I have no doubt that the 'energy' they refer to, which is used by so many cultures, is real, although it is known by many different names. The Russians have been researching it under the name of bioplasmic energy for many years and believe it is actually the electromagnetic field of the body. The same energy is used in acupuncture. The Hindus call it 'prana', the Chinese 'chi'.

The techniques I have observed during reiki training sessions being used to convince students that they have 'the power' to heal cover the full range of those described in Chapter 3, although the Masters' techniques vary according to the size of group they are teaching.

Fortune Tellers

Many people (myself included) have experienced very strong premonitions about the future which have turned out to be correct. There are many things that we don't understand about ourselves and our universe. Fortune telling isn't one of them. Next time you wonder if a fortune teller has special powers you might like to consider this explanation instead.

When you consult a fortune teller, the first thing they do usually is to touch you in some way. This invasion of your personal space immediately raises your level of arousal and consequently inhibits critical thinking (when you feel nervous it is difficult to think straight). As will be explained in

Chapter 3 this increases the possibility of another person accessing your right brain and the unconscious processes and beliefs it stores.

The next step by a fortune teller is to get you to focus your eyes on some object such as a crystal ball, or your own hand. This eye focusing puts you further into a receptive state for suggestion. The fortune teller then proceeds in a soft, comfortable and soothing voice to tell your future. What they are *really* doing is planting suggestions or programming your future while you are in a highly suggestive, even hypnotic state. Suggestions programmed into your unconscious can modify your future behaviour and your beliefs about yourself, resulting in the 'predictions' coming true.

Witches

A 'white' witch once told me that I should not confuse white witches with black witches. According to her, white witches cast spells to help people and black witches cast spells to harm people. The same witch told me she now called herself a 'metaphysicist' rather than a witch as it sounded more socially acceptable and scientific to people!

Whether a coven claims to be black or white, many of the psychological techniques and processes witches use are the same as those employed by cults, even if the aim of these processes is different, as my white witch claimed. White or black, witches use a great deal of ritual in their ceremonies. Sadly there are now some psychologists who are working almost full time helping people who are victims of ritual abuse.

The few people I have spoken to who have been victims

of ritual abuse all said that initially they thought joining a coven was a bit of harmless fun. Whether the rituals they took part in were black or white is often not clear, but some victims told me that they thought they were dealing with white witches. They were shocked and confused by how easily they became involved in more and more bizarre and damaging activities. Some suspected that at various times they had been drugged.

Rituals are extremely dangerous as they can be so hypnotic. The concentration necessary to get them right focuses the participant's attention completely, particularly when ritualistic actions are accompanied by rhythmic chanting and drumming. When the rituals are performed after fasts of many hours or even days they are even more potent. Once hypnotised by the ritual a participant is extremely vulnerable to being psychologically damaged.

Many people think that modern witches and covens are harmless or entertaining, and anyone who is adversely affected by them is simply weak, gullible or a fool. Nothing could be further from the truth! Witches' covens often attract people with a curiosity about natural healing and they may be quite level-headed. This does not prevent them being damaged.

Recently there has been a tremendous interest in 'fairies', as decoration on giftware, and in their significance in literature. What many people don't realise is that fairies were originally witches' little helpers. Black witches used 'black' or 'dark' fairies, and these were depicted as old, haggard and sinister. The fairies of our childhood stories were 'white', or good fairies, and depicted as pretty, smiling beings. If you walk into one of the fairy shops that have begun to appear make sure you are dealing with the white type. I have been warned of a fairy shop specialising in the old-hag kind of fairy that turned out to be a front for a black witches' coven!

In the last few years another type of witch has appeared. Although they often call themselves 'white witches' they seem to be quite different from the white witches I talked to twenty years ago. These new 'white witches' describe themselves as 'eco-feminists' and covens have come together in recent times made up of women disillusioned with the patriarchal system of Christian churches resistant to change. These women also reject many aspects of Christianity itself, such as the concept of heaven and hell. Hence the concept of Satan has no relevance to their beliefs, and practices society would consider evil are no part of their traditions.

Instead, these witches are often strong, even radical feminists. They celebrate their own power as women through an exploration of pre-Christian (usually Celtic) goddesses. They combine this with ancient and modern beliefs about women (and men) being part of the environment (not separate from it) and therefore much of their worship involves rituals to do with seasonal changes and the movement of the earth, moon and stars.

Eco-witches do not believe in or participate in drug taking or sacrificial ceremonies. Nevertheless, like orthodox religions many of their techniques can cause changes in arousal and therefore suggestible states. Eco-witches are a very loose network of women, with varying ways of exploring and expressing their beliefs, so it can be extremely difficult for people interested in pursuing a harmless (and even environmentally sound) belief to be sure of whom they are dealing with. Be extremely careful when choosing your coven!

MULTI-LEVEL MARKETING

Sales people have been among the first to start using psychological techniques to manipulate people (see 'Use of Language and Body Cues', pages 86–90). Usually you know if someone is selling a product, so you are prepared and therefore cautious. Increasingly people are being manoeuvred into joining very large group gatherings where they are processed through powerful psychological techniques to sell them something, when they thought they were just attending an 'information evening'. One marketing group used group hypnosis to make people fire-walk and then immediately afterwards, while they were still in a highly aroused state, got them to sign expensive business contracts to learn to become teachers of fire-walking themselves!

One of the best known multi-level marketing organisations is Amway. This hugely successful company started selling soap powder and now in some countries even sells cars. In order to make the most money in Amway, or to be truly 'successful', it is necessary to move 'upline' by recruiting more and more distributors like yourself, who themselves recruit distributors and so on. You make money not just from the goods you sell but by getting a percentage of what the distributors you have recruited sell as well.

As with all sales and marketing jobs, this requires extremely hard work and high motivation. Increasingly

Amway is adopting similar techniques to many cults in order to attract recruits, then to keep them involved and committed to the cause. For instance Amway distributors are instructed not to tell you they are selling Amway up front. Usually you are asked to attend a meeting about an 'exciting new business opportunity'. In fact Amway's name may not be mentioned until after a good hour of sales pitch.

The approach of the marketing organisation is usually quite evangelical. It asks if there is something missing in your life, and offers all sorts of emotional inducements: 'reach your full potential', 'find the real you', 'gain greater meaning and more meaningful relationships in your life'. In many ways Amway is more like a fundamentalist religion than a direct marketing business, with money as the god. Joining Amway is often described, by its distributors, as like a religious or spiritual experience.

Distributors are encouraged to recruit first amongst their family and friends, an action that can very quickly put open, trusting relationships on a very shaky footing as friendship is exploited for financial gain. Amway distributors become aware of where a potential recruit is emotionally most vulnerable by asking questions like 'What do you want out of life? or 'What is missing from your life?' Friendships and relationships are further abused when the target tries to say no. The Amway distributor may turn this into a personal rejection of himself, and the recruit can be made to feel guilty that he or she is turning a friend down.

Many people have told me about relationships they valued highly that were never quite the same after they tried to recruit a friend or family member to Amway. A side effect of this is that a new Amway distributor very quickly becomes dependent on other distributors 'who think the same', for friendship as well as business relationships.

Amway encourages more and more dependence on the Amway family and its values. For instance, a distributor told me about Amway's recommendations to deal with problems in marriage (because of the demands Amway places on a partner's time and priorities!). He said Amway suggested it was not a good idea to consult a professional marriage counsellor, who would probably not understand how Amway worked. Instead marriage and personal problems should be be dealt with in-house by going 'upline' to an Amway distributor at a higher level!

This deliberately restricts a distributor's emotional resources to Amway and its particular value system – one which sees wives only as their husbands' assistants, and regards men as being the sole decision-makers in marriage. Books and tapes are produced targeted directly at Amway wives and the role they are expected to play.

To keep distributors involved and active, weekly meetings are held where people are encouraged to talk about personal as well as business difficulties. The 'upline' distributor – the one who has recruited others and therefore takes a percentage of their sales – functions as a priest, to whom failures to fulfil Amway commitments and expectations can be confessed and absolved, and further commitments made as a way of paying penance.

Extremely large gatherings are held regularly (sometimes as often as monthly) and at these many of the techniques used by traditional cults are employed to reinforce values and enhance commitment, for instance, confessions, success sharing and singing. Participants are expected to conform to a strict dress code: jacket and tie for men, smart dresses and jackets for women – no pants!

Many people hearing about the deliberately manipulative techniques used by multi-level marketing groups shrug their shoulders and say 'So what?'. Unfortunately dropping out of Amway and similar groups may not be simple or totally harmless. In the present economic climate people who have been retrenched are turning desperately to Amway to find some kind of income. Because of their situation they are often extremely vulnerable emotionally and Amway uses this mercilessly. A typical recruitment pitch would include the phrases 'Do you have the courage to make significant changes in your life?', 'Do this for your children's sake', 'Our only failures are quitters,' and 'Doesn't your family deserve what Amway can give them [materially]?'

Such highly charged language, when aimed at vulnerable people in large groups and backed up with a constant stream of audio tapes which 'those who are truly committed to success will use conscientiously and diligently', can be extremely effective. But if you are not a whiz-bang seller, consider personal relationships above money, and everybody you know was signed up for Amway long ago, then it is very easy to 'fail' at Amway. Coming on top of retrenchment, the resultant self-doubt and the guilt that Amway plays on can cause great distress and real depression. One ex-Amway wife told me: 'My marriage, which was struggling along on a minimal income due to Joe's [husband] retrenchment, couldn't survive a dose of Amway as well.'

There are many multi-level marketing schemes operating, not just Amway. Some demand a huge financial outlay from recruits in order to become distributors – but they give no guarantees that there will not be 100 000 other distributorships in the same city.

If you are introduced into a direct marketing scheme that does not demand control of your lifestyle, relationships and values, then maybe it can be a satisfying job. But beware those that offer 'not just a career but a way of life'. Read the description of recruitment techniques in Chapter 3 carefully so that you can recognise when a sales pitch is using these covert methods.

FUNDAMENTALISTS

Fundamentalism in Religion

Fundamentalists are people who believe in the literal truth of the Bible, the Koran or any other set of written beliefs. The rise of fundamentalist groups in recent times is not surprising. People who are unsure of themselves and confused by conflicting values in society can latch on to a set of rules or basic (fundamental) 'truths' to live their life by, as a way of making some sort of sense of conflicting ideas, events and experiences.

The problem of course is that even if the Bible or Koran *is* the word of God, it has been translated and passed down through the ages by human beings, with errors and changing interpretations becoming entrenched. Fundamentalists however still persist in literal interpretation, which reduces every ethical question to a black and white issue. Unfortunately real, modern life is rarely black and white but an infinite grey.

People struggling to find firm values are often attracted

to the simplistic view of life held by fundamentalists. Its appeal is made even greater because fundamentalists are now using many of the techniques mentioned in this book to manipulate beliefs of converts and maintain their compliance.

Young people are frequently searching hard for meaning in their lives. The psychological recruitment techniques are most effective on young people, as the younger the subject the easier it is to manipulate their belief systems (see Chapter 3) so it is not surprising that fundamentalist religions using them are the fastest growing religious groups in our community.

Fundamentalist religions also tend to prey on people in the middle of a life crisis, such as bereavement or illness. Members of the church may go to extraordinary lengths to do thoughtful deeds and give practical help at that time. They know full well that a kindness done when the recipient is upset and thus emotionally vulnerable will have a powerful impact and increase the chances that the person will turn to them if he or she needs help again.

Many people think that as long as the converts seem happy in these religions the situation is not a worry. However, such sects' fundamentalist attitudes can have profound consequences on wider society as members begin to gain positions of influence. For instance, some fundamentalist religions regard women as men's helpers, subservient and in practice definitely not equal in marriage relationships. Other sects are aggressive campaigners to have abortion again made illegal.

If members were acquiring their beliefs in an environment of critical evaluation of the issues then I would not be concerned, but the recruitment techniques of cults are increasingly being used by fundamentalist religions to deliberately dampen down people's ability to evaluate thoroughly the beliefs being taught to them. The same techniques are then used to maintain compliance with the belief system.

Fundamentalist Political Groups

In some countries fundamentalist political groups have strong links with fundamentalist religions. Many people who grew up in fundamentalist religions are attracted to the simplicity of fundamentalist politics, where all society's problems can be reduced to simple theoretical economic models and principles, without having to bother too much with that elusive 'human factor'. But fundamentalist politics are not confined to religious societies. During the 1980s much of the democratic world was governed by political parties who espoused fundamentalist economic theories. It is now being finally recognised that simplistic models of managing economies – privatisation, economic rationalism, free markets – have had catastrophic results economically and socially in Britain, New Zealand and the United States of America.

How do politicians manage to initiate major shifts in policy? A great deal of intensive research has been done in recent years on how successful speakers present both themselves and their material. A 'successful' speaker is defined as one who can cause a change in the attitudes and beliefs of the audience. The results of such analyses are now widely used to maximise the effectiveness of politicians, particularly when dealing with the media.

One of the most powerful ways of doing this is in the speaker's use of verbal and body language. The language used by a politician can profoundly affect his or her ability to persuade an audience or reach them emotionally. In advertising (and particularly political advertising) the best way of reaching your audience is to achieve an emotional reaction. For example, in the recent Australian federal elections Paul Keating's Labor government was re-elected despite all odds. His effectiveness in persuading the electorate to vote for him was greatly enhanced by his natural ability (perhaps made more potent by coaching), to use what are actually neuro-linguistic programming (NLP) language techniques. To give an image of what Australian society would be like under a Hewson Liberal government he used phrases such as 'a society ripping and tearing itself apart' and 'people grabbing and clawing over each other'. These words are rich in semantic density, providing instant pictures and emotional responses. He described life in Australia under his government as 'caring and sharing', 'reaching down to help others less able'. The words were backed by strong body language, with his hands demonstrating ripping and tearing actions in the first instance, and reaching down with one arm and in a gentle voice acting out helping someone up in the second.

John Hewson, on the other hand, used very dry economic language and held rallies that were often portrayed in the news coverage as upsetting and confrontational with his opponents – which unwittingly supported exactly what Paul Keating was describing.

Senior members of the Liberal Party itself acknowledged

in their election post-mortem that John Hewson's use of language was a problem and that it would have to be 'addressed'. In the months since the election there has been a noticeable difference in the kind of language that John Hewson uses.

Because of the power of these NLP techniques now in use, especially when employed in political advertising on television and radio, true discussion of issues is avoided. My view is that in a real democracy we cannot afford to have our election campaigns reduced to emotive language and misleading, short, attention-grabbing slogans. I feel very strongly, and many in the advertising industry itself agree with me, that if we are to have any hope of future governments being elected on the basis of a rational debate about important issues then all electronic political advertising should be banned – not as an infringement of free speech but in order that true free speech is maintained. *Free speech does not exist when that speech is given in a way that deliberately inhibits the listener's critical evaluation of what is being said.*

THREE

How Beliefs are Manipulated

In order to understand the overall psychological process involved in changing perceptions and beliefs it is necessary to understand how the brain functions.

The higher cortex of the brain is made up of two halves, or hemispheres: the left hemisphere (on the left side of the body) and the right hemisphere (on the right side of the body). They are joined together by connective tissue known as the corpus callosum. This connection is extremely important as it allows the hemispheres to co-ordinate thinking and action. Generally speaking the left hemisphere controls the right side of the body and the right hemisphere controls the left side of the body.

The hemispheres operate rather differently. The left brain thinks logically and sequentially. It is self-centred and critical, seeing things in symbolic form. It likes to be analytical and view the world in terms of its component parts like a machine. The right brain is co-operative and more ecological in its thinking. It thinks in patterns, looking at the overall picture. It is more creative, able to take information and look at it in new and different ways.

If the corpus callosum is cut surgically (this was done

as an early treatment for grand mal epilepsy before appropriate drugs became available) then rather bizarre behaviour can result. One man who had this surgery found it cured his epilepsy but he once discovered one hand buttoning up his shirt as the other hand undid the buttons! His left, logical brain was making his right hand do up the buttons because he was dutifully dressing for work, whereas his right brain (which appears to have greater access to our unconscious thoughts) was making the left hand undo them because deep down he really didn't want to go to work!

Studying many other patients who have had surgery or brain damage from strokes and accidents has also revealed that the hemispheres function differently in men and women. In men the left brain tends to be strongly dominant over the right. In women the left brain is still the dominant one, but their right brain is far more active and more easily accessible than men's.

The right hemisphere appears to have direct access to our unconscious processes and emotions. Its role is to take information provided by our senses, from around and within us, and try to make sense of it by creating meaningful patterns. The pattern is then presented to the left brain for critical review to see how it checks out with previous experiences and information. If it is consistent with previous experiences it can be easily incorporated into our existing beliefs. If it is not consistent then the left, critical brain will become cautious and demand more information, or an adaptation of the right brain's pattern, in order to accept this new material. The left critical brain acts a bit like a devil's advocate to make sure new beliefs will work with existing beliefs, rules and responsibilities.

We can thus understand why beliefs are so important biologically and psychologically to human beings. From the time we are tiny babies we are taking in information with our senses, sorting it into a pattern and then checking the pattern with our left brain to see whether it is consistent with earlier beliefs we have developed about the world. Without building up such a system of beliefs about our physical and emotional environment we would have to relearn from scratch with every experience and could not build on past knowledge.

For this reason the developing brain and central nervous system of a child functions quite differently to that of an adult. In children the right brain is less dominated by the left one, and the right brain constantly explores its world and makes sense of it by creating patterns. The full critical powers of the left brain do not develop until much later in life, so children are far more vulnerable than adults to techniques aimed at manipulating their beliefs.

If you look at the traditional hypnotherapy of indigenous people in Africa, Australia, South America and America and the more recent hypnosis techniques developed by Milton Erikson and Erni Rossi using the mindbody connection (ideodynamic techniques), then hypnosis can generally be described as a process by which the activity of the left brain (critical, logical analysis) is dampened down in order to give greater access to the right brain. Under hypnosis your unconscious processes can be manipulated in order to change your perceptions and beliefs about yourself and the world you live in. As explained earlier, hypnosis does *not* mean the subject is necessarily in a trance-like or sleepwalking state.

The special hypnotic state is not just psychological; it also produces physical changes – especially within the endogenous opiate system of the body. This is a chemical system that controls the level and type of opiates produced by the body and circulating around it. Opiates are substances chemically similar to morphine, pethidine and heroin. They are the body's own way of controlling pain and giving pleasurable feelings. The role of this system in the body is probably extremely important in understanding the behaviour of victims of cults, and the relationships they have with their leaders or gurus.

While people are participating in many of the psychological techniques and activities used by cults and groups, their endogenous opiate levels apparently change, giving them a euphoric buzz or feeling of being really alive. Participants often leave sessions on an incredible high. Cults, groups and gurus are quick to claim credit for these feelings, saying it is their particular technique, magic or personal energy that is giving the participants these wonderful, powerful feelings. In fact, under similar psychological and physical conditions one could recite nursery rhymes or nonsense and still attain the high feeling at the end of the session. Sessions are deliberately designed to induce high levels of arousal because this makes it easier to manipulate beliefs.

The high can last many days, sometimes weeks, but as the opiate level returns to normal some people can suffer withdrawal symptoms similar to those felt by athletes whose bodies have got used to a very high level of opiates in hard training and who then suddenly stop exercising, possibly because of injury. This withdrawal can cause fatigue, depression, a flat feeling, or even physical symptoms like headaches, nausea and pains in the joints.

In order to feel better many people seek out their guru or group leader, who usually tells them that it is a 'healing crisis'. He gives them another dose of techniques that will induce the psycho-physiological state necessary to create more opiates and they begin to feel better. Someone can become addicted very quickly to these psycho-physiological processes (or rather, to the opiates they produce) and suffer real drug withdrawal if they cease to participate. People addicted to personal development courses are commonly referred to as 'seminar junkies'. Such a physical addiction is probably one of the reasons people trying to leave cults find it so hard and tend to return to them, even when they are very unhappy.

A similar process may well be contributing to the 'battered wives' syndrome'. Outsiders find it extremely hard to understand why a woman will stay with a violent man and suffer continual emotional and physical abuse. In this situation the woman lives in a constant state of very high arousal, because of the totally unpredictable and contradictory nature of the man's behaviour (one minute extremely loving, the next very violent). This makes it difficult for her to think clearly or critically about the situation or abuse she is being subjected to. Because the man (as cult leaders and gurus do to sect members in a more subtle way) constantly tells the woman she is making mistakes or not fulfilling expectations (disobeying rules, is not 'committed enough') the woman (or group member) comes to believe that it is *her* inadequacy that determines the husband's (leader's) attitude and behaviour to her. If only she (or the group member) was less dumb (more committed) the husband (leader) would have no reason to disapprove of them or to 'chastise' them.

This type of 'logic' neatly shifts the responsibility for abuse from the abuser to the victim. In the victims' state of foggy thinking and heightened arousal they become addicted physically and emotionally to a situation they think *they* are controlling.

I hope that now I have explained a little about how modern hypnosis works (fuller details of the actual techniques follow in the next section), I will have caused some concern about who is allowed to use these techniques and under what conditions. Unfortunately no state in Australia has *effective* controls on hypnosis. Those that do, really only deal with the more traditional methods of hypnosis. Even in those states where some restrictions apply the only people who are in effect restricted in what they do are the registered professionals! Anybody else in the community can get away with using hypnosis as long as they don't call it that.

Many people practising these modern techniques are not even aware that they are using hypnosis. They are genuinely confused and surprised when bad or dangerous reactions occur. The problem is that if someone doesn't have proper training they will not know enough to recognise the possible dangers, or when and how to use appropriate safeguards. Unfortunately in some states there is now a proliferation of 'hypnotherapy schools' being set up, by people who themselves may have no proper training in hypnosis. If you would like to see a properly trained hypnotherapist the only reliable Australia-wide register is with the Australian Society of Hypnosis, c/o Austin Hospital, Heidelberg, Victoria 3084.

The following pages contain an overview of the various techniques used to inhibit one's ability to think critically, that is, to put someone in a receptive state, in order to access and change their beliefs and unconscious frameworks. If done without consent such poking around in someone's unconscious can wreak havoc with their convictions and attitudes, and cause general mayhem in their private life.

The techniques are currently used by cults, personal development groups, sales operations and fundamentalist religions. They are presented here in the order in which they tend to be used by groups or cults, but they may be used in various combinations. Participants will rarely be exposed to all of them, for only one or two may be needed to be effective.

Broadly speaking the techniques aim to change beliefs by changing an individual's behaviour, physical state, thoughts and perceptions about himself or herself and the world around, and their consequent emotional responses to situations and people.

RECRUITMENT

Recruitment into cults or to attend personal development courses can be extremely open: through advertising in the print media, or on shopfronts. It may also be done in a very obscure way that makes it difficult to identify the group and their intentions properly until one is already heavily involved. If you are answering an advertisement or decide to attend a 'centre' offering personal growth courses, try and find out as much as you possibly can *before* you attend (see Chapter 6).

Some groups hold meetings or lectures with vague but idealistic titles that may be openly advertised, for instance, 'World Peace', 'How to Make Your World Happy' or 'Cosmic Consciousness'. Other groups run all sorts of courses that help them screen out people not suitable for their purposes and pick the vulnerable ones for recruitment. The process of recruitment begins as you become involved in the course and you reveal more and more information about yourself to its leader.

Door-to-door selling of goods for cash – chocolates, flowers – not only raises funds but can act as an ice-breaker, the seller pinpointing people who are vulnerable. Often door-knockers quite blatantly ask for money for some worthy-sounding cause – always check their credentials before donating money.

Many organisations seek out vulnerable people in the centre of cities, at train and bus stations and airports. They offer help and friendship to those who appear alone. Typically the person making the approach will seem to be the kindest, most caring, sweetest person imaginable, and may not seem quite 'real'. Recruiters also tend to stand very close to their targets, deliberately invading their personal space. The Moonies used a particularly cunning ploy: they would appear to be perfectly normal and offer people who looked isolated advice about being careful of 'cult groups that sometimes hang around here'. This would immediately make *them* seem safe to the potential victim.

Cults and groups are very adept at discovering the particular kind of approach that will work best with different kinds of people. The Moonies considered people to be of four basic types: Feelers, Believers, Thinkers and Doers. The cult would be marketed to the potential recruit in a way that would appeal most to their personality.

'Thinkers' were intellectual types who would be attracted to the ideas and philosophies of the group and would be stimulated by meeting other thinkers. 'Thinkers' would be encouraged to attend lectures given by well-known speakers, who although being paid to speak by the cult might not have actually been members themselves. 'Feelers' were considered to be people needing love, acceptance, and family-type activities from the group. 'Doers' were those who would be attracted by the idea of 'helping the world' in practical ways and 'Believers' were people wanting a God or spiritual meaning in their life.

These categories are still used by many groups today, but the categorisation of potential recruits is now enhanced by much more sophisticated techniques that use the person's body cues and language style (NLP) to analyse the most effective way of recruiting them.

Very quickly after a person becomes involved with a group it will be suggested to them, or they will be instructed, to start actively recruiting others. This is deliberately done so that the person becomes more and more convinced himself or herself of the correctness of the group's answers every time he or she tries to convince others.

COMMITMENT

One of the most common methods used by cults, groups and gurus to inhibit recruits from critically analysing what they are doing is to build commitment into the way people join the group. Then they set intermittent tests of this commitment.

Running 'courses' immediately legitimises demands for a monetary commitment. Course charges can be anything from a few dollars to several thousand, but whatever their size, they are a way of immediately committing the person paying to the group's program and beliefs. Once the course starts it is highly unlikely that participants will question their own judgement and face the possibility that they may not be getting their money's worth, or even that they have been conned.

Nor are people likely to question the group or guru if they have committed themselves – especially when any question or criticism is turned back on to the participant to question their 'commitment'. Typical responses from leaders to worries raised by participants are:

'You don't appear to be really committed here?'
'Perhaps you're not ready for the commitment needed to benefit from us?'
'As you become more committed things will become clearer.'

These questions of 'commitment' are used to imply that the participant is inadequate in some way, rather than the course. They also imply – as does the body language used by the leader – that questioners aren't really part of the committed group yet.

This subtle rejection by a group who seem to have the secret of success, peace of mind or whatever, is very hard to accept while one is isolated with the group, so recruits start to try harder to prove their commitment. At first, this may be by simply not questioning what is being said, but later it may mean fully participating in the group's activities to regain approval.

Subtle, manipulative put-downs may also be used to commit people further:

'Of course it takes *real courage* to change yourself.' (Implies that if you resist change you are a coward.)

'Some people can't accept they don't know everything.' (Implies you are a know-all if you question what is being said or done.)

'If you were really committed you wouldn't ask questions about money or where it goes. You would trust us. Perhaps you have a problem with trust?'

The level of insecurity that follows questioning is so intense that the participant stops analysing the situation logically and accepts the cult's line in order to defuse the situation.

GUILT

Challenging your level of commitment basically works by making you feel guilty. You feel guilt when you think you have broken some extremely important rule. In this case the unspoken rule is: 'I must be totally "committed" to whatever happens here regardless of my previous values and beliefs'.

All cults, groups and courses, such as the ones I'm talking about here, have large numbers of written and unwritten rules. The more rules they have and the more pervasively they affect your life (such as rules about diet, break times, work or attitudes) the more difficult it becomes to accept or adhere to the rules without breaking some. Breaking the rules (or even thinking about breaking them) creates guilt, and the more guilt created the greater is the fear in the participant or member, and the greater the power and control of the group or leader.

The Roman Catholic Church is an institution based on guilt and the concept of confession and absolution. The behaviour of the old-style Christian Brothers in their schools has unfortunately resulted in an incredible amount of work for me as a psychologist over the years. But at least the Christian Brothers and the Roman Catholic Church generally are now recognising and doing something about the human abuses of their religion – they themselves acknowledge their accountability to the wider community, and the Church has even accepted responsibility for the behaviour of priests who are paedophiles.

Christian fundamentalist religions also use guilt extensively as a way of controlling members and testing their commitment. Fundamentalist rules are so black and white they are often just not appropriate or realistic in real life. Members of the church who question – or break – rules because they cannot be applied to real situations (for instance, the issue of whether abortion should be available to a young girl who has been raped) feel guilty, and the power of the church is reasserted over them.

CHANGING LEVEL OF AROUSAL

As discussed earlier, before someone can inhibit your ability to evaluate information, behaviour and activities critically, it is necessary for them to change your level of arousal. This will in turn give the leader greater access to your right brain in order to change or modify your beliefs, and access your unconscious processes.

People often wonder why recruits don't just revert to the beliefs they originally held when the seminar is over or they leave a cult. However in order to change beliefs it is necessary to replicate the psycho-physiological state in which they first developed. This is a built-in brain mechanism that ensures beliefs continue to be perceived as valid in an appropriate context. For instance, a young child encountering a large black shape in a back yard that snarls and bites will develop a belief that large black shapes can be dangerous. Each time a large black shape is encountered in the future there is a high probability that a similar psycho-physiological state will be induced and the child will decide that the situation is dangerous because he or she is in the state where the 'danger' signal was learnt. It will be quite difficult to change that belief unless a similar state is induced in which the child experiences large black shapes that can be friendly and fun.

Groups of all kinds, but particularly those with a defined leader or guru, commonly create situations in which the participant is treated like a child and the leader takes the role of parent. This parent/child approach, together with other techniques, can recreate quite nicely the psycho-physiological states that occurred when beliefs were acquired in childhood. The participant is being put into a state where their fundamental beliefs can be changed.

Methods used to vary levels of arousal can differ between groups, or one group may use different methods at different times. The most effective processes employ both decreases and increases in arousal, and some of the most common ways of changing arousal are now described in detail.

Attention Focusing

Groups often make you focus your mind on some idea, symbolic sound or object. Mantras are a favourite device: these are simple sounds repeated over and over. Some groups claim your mantra is especially designed for you (this justifies the high costs of the course!) and will lose its power if you divulge it. At a party one night a group of people I knew who were deeply involved in a meditation group got a bit tipsy. One brave soul risked losing the power of his mantra and confided it to his friend. This put everyone into a secret-disclosing mood and they were furious to find that their expensive mantras were all the same!

Altered states of arousal also occur with visual focusing, for instance when people focus their eyes on some fixed or moving point. This can be as simple as focusing closely on a speaker. To enhance this effect speakers at meetings are often put under spotlights, or the audience is asked to focus on a fire or candles, or a symbolic object like a cross, statue or picture.

Lighting

Lighting, sometimes patterns of different colours and of varying intensity, is used very effectively in most groups to change arousal levels. The light may be subdued or extremely bright, flickering candles or strobe lights. Lighting can be particularly effective at causing disorientation and time distortion – where time seems to pass extremely quickly or slowly. Time distortion is a phenomenon commonly experienced in hypnotic states.

Music and Sounds

There has been a lot of research in the last few years into the physical and psychological effects of sounds on people, particularly rhythms and beats.

Many ancient cultures considered music such a powerful influence that playing musical instruments, and even their tuning, was restricted to designated members of religious orders. Particular kinds of Indian music were designed specifically to create and balance certain states in the mind and body, even at different times of the day. The ancient Greeks and Romans used music and sounds to heal wounds and cure illness.

Using sound as a way to change arousal varies from imposing total silence (as in sensory deprivation chambers or flotation tanks), or repeating single sounds to focus attention, to chanting, singing and producing different voice modulations, especially in a slow monotone, or rhythmic sounds like drums. Stirring classical or hard rock music is commonly used by cults and fundamentalist religions to increase the level of arousal. Slow music, of about sixty beats per minute, can induce decreased arousal and trance-like states very quickly.

Masking music or wave sounds are used on subliminal tapes to hide embedded messages that are said to be able to gain access to your unconscious without you being aware of what the messages are saying. These tapes are commonly advertised for use to aid weight loss, stop smoking, increase self-esteem and to promote relaxation. The research on their effectiveness is controversial. Tapes can cost $50 or more, and some have been found to contain no messages at all!

Tapes to 'synchronise' the right and left hemispheres of the brain are now one of the latest fashions in psychotherapists' electronic wizardry. These tapes claim to create relaxation and peace of mind, and to increase creativity. They are being produced by a variety of people, some well-respected professionals but also some complete amateurs. There is no doubt that a great deal of exciting research is being done at present into psychological techniques such as these. However the results I see from people coming to see me who have used such tapes vary from them having had no effect, or sometimes profound improvement in the area they focused on, through to increased anxiety and actual panic attacks. I suspect that these tapes can have an effect but they really need to be individually prescribed for patients, to avoid triggering unconscious processes that can create havoc with their emotional well-being.

This is especially true of the ordinary audio tapes widely available by mail order, in health food stores and New Age shops, that have verbal instructions on them, not just music. People have complained to me of symptoms they have developed while listening to apparently harmless tapes on relaxation, self-esteem or healing. This is not surprising. The tapes are rarely made by people trained in ideodynamic hypnosis techniques and, without realising it, they may use inappropriate visualisations and language.

Seating

Seating is often used as a way of rewarding compliance and commitment, and of controlling recruits' behaviour. There may be special seating reserved for existing 'followers', which surrounds the seating of newcomers. If a newcomer asks questions about what is being said or done they often 'feel' the concentrated eyes of all the followers sitting behind focused on them. Often one or two followers will come and actually sit beside the questioner, which inhibits him or her from asking further questions, or the newcomer finds themselves during or after a break surrounded and engaged in conversation by a number of existing followers. This can be done in a friendly, caring way initially but may become hostile if the person doesn't shut up.

Restrictive and uncomfortable seating is used by some groups to deliberately produce fatigue, which leads to changes in arousal. People may not be able to leave the room (even to go to the toilet!) once a 'session' has started and these sessions can continue without breaks for many hours (if a participant needs to leave they may be accused of 'resisting' or made to feel very guilty). If someone complains about the seating or fidgets they may also be accused of resisting and not having sufficient commitment. Some groups ask participants to remove watches and stop the clocks, to increase the possibility of their experiencing time distortion and disorientation. These techniques have been commonly reported by people attending seminars run by Landmark Education (this group has been known previously as both Forum and EST), Money and You and Reiki.

Other groups use extremely comfortable seating, or have the participants reclining in beanbags on the floor in a very warm room, and this also causes changed arousal. Some lengthy seminars vary between the two techniques.

Emotional Atmosphere

If you meet a group of people who seem to be the most peaceful, enlightened, loving, accepting, positive, caring people you could possibly imagine then be suspicious! Be especially wary if they seem to be constantly smiling and invading your personal space by standing too close or touching you unnecessarily.

Superficially everything may seem wonderful, but if anyone seriously questions the leader's beliefs, actions or instructions, then watch out! The group can turn supernasty very quickly. When challenged by a recruit, ridicule, intimidation, rejection, and verbal abuse are commonly used to control that person. In cults this often extends to physical abuse, which is considered to be 'good for them'.

Sometimes the leader, or his off-sider, will deliberately pick an argument or insult someone they suspect of not being compliant enough. This verbal assault dramatically increases the victim's arousal, their ability to think critically becomes negligible and in order to avoid further assault they comply with the leader. Bullying may be made even more effective by isolating the victim in a special place in front of the group – a 'hot seat'.

Creating a highly charged emotional atmosphere directly targets the right side of the brain and its unconscious processes. (Advertisers have known for years that the most effective advertising causes an emotional, not a logical response.)

Touching

Sadly, many people in our community are starved of loving human contact through touching. People who touch others very little will be highly aroused emotionally by physical contact. This can be abused in groups very easily by making people feel inadequate, inhibited and uncommitted (that word again!) if they resist touching and hugging sessions that invade their personal space. Learning to touch comfortably can be an important step for people who need to learn how to trust, but an issue of this kind needs to be dealt with by professionals who really know what they are doing and who have the interests of the *person* as their highest priority – not the needs of a group or its leader.

Cults sometimes use nudity as 'tests' of a person's commitment and willingness to humble themselves – and literally bare all to the leader or the group. More common though are sudden demands for recruits to turn to perfect strangers and give them a hug. There is no faster way of increasing the level of your arousal and inhibiting critical thinking than having your personal space invaded by a stranger.

Another hug, the 'power' hug, is often used by cults and groups to subdue dissidents in the ranks. This involves the leader placing his or her arms over the top of the dissident's so that the latter cannot break the hug first. When the hug is broken is decided by the leader, hence establishing his or her position of power over the follower.

Massage is of wonderful benefit to people emotionally and physically but unfortunately it can be easily abused. It is common for people to enter light trance states quite spontaneously during massage, when their unconscious minds may be accessible to the masseur. If during a massage the masseur starts talking about your private life and giving you suggestions, or starts discussing his own belief system, this can trigger a great deal of confusion or actually influence your own beliefs. Choose masseurs who let you explore the lovely feelings of light trance on your own, or who keep to safe topics such as the weather. If a masseur starts to dabble in your private and emotional life it would be safer to find another one!

Massage is often abused by groups, who make it an excuse to get people's clothes off. Nudity in public is an unusual state, and one that can make you very vulnerable emotionally. Be extremely wary of any suggestions along such lines.

If you wish to learn massage then contact the Consumer Affairs department in your state to check on the massage school before enrolling, and be alert to any teachers who may be abusing their positions. One woman who contacted me said she had discovered that a massage course called 'Postural Integration' was actually a screening device for recruiting new members to the Sannyassin cult.

Crowd Arousal

Anyone who has attended a huge rock concert or a football final can remember the extraordinary 'high' one gets from being in such a large group of people with a common interest. It is a wonderful feeling to participate in an event where the power of masses of people is united in a common aim. Even though you are only in the audience there is a sense of excitement and anticipation that puts you into a highly aroused state where clear thinking can be impossible.

Hitler knew, and used, the power of the mass rally instinctively. More recently May Day rallies in Moscow and Beijing have used this crowd euphoria quite deliberately to create a powerful sense of belonging to a society with set beliefs and ideals. American politicians have been using it increasingly in organised rallies during their presidential campaigns.

Armies put men in uniform to give them a collective identity, where the needs of the individual are subservient to the needs of the common cause. The marching beat of military music is no accident. It has rhythm and emphases that merge easily with the rhythm of the body movements of a march, and thus it unites the marchers in a common repetitive rhythm that can be quite hypnotic.

Ever since Hitler used propaganda so formidably, there has been detailed analysis of his methods. The effects of crowd arousal, symbolism and the use of particular kinds of language have been studied – and the results used extensively by advertisers, sales people and politicians. These techniques are also used by cults, gurus and group leaders. Some people ('born leaders' and 'born salesmen') have a natural tendency to use manipulative techniques quite unconsciously. These are people generally perceived by others to be charming and persuasive. Increasingly these behaviour patterns are being learnt and are then being used to deliberately manipulate the behaviour and beliefs of an unsuspecting public.

Very large groups – of several hundred or more – are now being manipulated by gurus, cults and personal development courses, but the group size will vary depending on the aim of the organisation or guru. The leaders consistently appeal to the audience through emotional triggers (affecting the right side of the brain) while dampening down the listeners' left-brain critical thinking, and thus huge shifts in the personal belief systems and values of the audience can occur even within one session – or sometimes even with one 'lecture' or 'information evening'.

If you attend a large meeting – whether it is an introduction to a new kind of business venture, a promise of ways to become a millionaire, or an obvious personal development course – in a large group you are subjected to a *very* powerful psychological process, the results of which may be quite unpredictable for any particular individual. It is important to remember that the buzz you may feel is a result of the group arousal phenomenon and the techniques being used, *not* what is necessarily being said or sold.

Residential Groups
These are potentially extremely dangerous – even more than large group meetings – as a person is isolated from his or her normal resources and is therefore *much more* dependent

on the approval of the group and its leader than someone attending an 'information evening'.

Most residential courses are held in relatively isolated locations, so that great physical dependence is immediately created, especially if all the participants are bussed together to the venue. Often participants are instructed to arrive at night, which adds to disorientation and therefore dependency.

Isolated from all the usual reference points of values, such as family, friends and normal responsibilities, it is much easier to shed old beliefs. Unfortunately, because the situation is not 'real', beliefs acquired on such retreats often don't work very well back in real life – they work best in the artificial environment of the group. Therefore people start to go back to do more courses, or live and work with the group, as that is the only way the new values and beliefs feel comfortable. The conflicts that may be created with spouses and former relationships are rationalised by the leaders as evidence that the recruits have moved 'beyond' these people.

Always check out the *appropriateness* of the qualifications of those running residential courses, and their degree of *accountability*, extremely carefully before attending such a course. For instance, if the course is about human relations or personal development, discover what *recognised* qualifications the leader has in this area (see also Chapter 6). Are teachers registered, or accountable in any way if something goes wrong?

There are many people who believe they have found the answers to life's problems for themselves physically and/or emotionally, or have recovered from life-threatening illnesses, who are now setting up shop as experts running residential courses in healing, personal growth or diet. Some of these people have 'qualifications': for instance, Ian Gawler of the 'Ian Gawler Foundation' is a vet who began running residential groups for cancer patients, although his courses are now aimed increasingly at people without cancer. Does his training as a vet qualify him to run intensive residential courses where people confront themselves and their relationships in an extremely intense way, often using the techniques of hypnosis?

The specific aim of the techniques Gawler uses at his residential retreats is to raise emotional and psychological issues that he believes to be the cause of patients' cancers or problems. This is potentially very dangerous territory being explored, in highly vulnerable people, by someone who may have the best of intentions but who has no training or accountability if something goes wrong. It is very easy to raise issues, but it is *not necessarily therapeutic*, especially if the person does not have immediate access to highly skilled and expert help to help them cope with unearthed problems. Since the Ian Gawler Foundation started residential courses I have seen people who were very confused and distraught over 'revelations' and issues raised at these courses that had not been properly resolved then.

The Ian Gawler Foundation originated many years ago from Ian's willingness to share what he had learned himself about meditation, and his extraordinary and wonderful conquering of his own cancer. The foundation ran courses just in meditation, and at that time I referred many people to it.

It has been with dismay that I have seen the organisation grow from one offering training in meditation to one that is now a considerable business, employing Ian and his wife full-time, selling a range of courses and products including intense personal 'growth' courses, extreme dietary regimes and vitamin and mineral supplements.

The Gawler Foundation is by no means the only or worst offender: other courses, like Hoffman Process, are run by people very skilled in marketing and sales, but with no qualifications which acknowledge them as recognised experts in the field they are teaching – except those given to them by the organisations themselves.

Diet

Diet is a very sophisticated technique for manipulating arousal levels. It has long been used in religious orders, but is now being increasingly used in seminars and residential workshops.

In some seminars meal or snack breaks are kept to a minimum – or the participants may be given food and drink that provide high levels of simple carbohydrates, such as biscuits, chocolate, sweets and sugary cordials. A high level of simple carbohydrate (carbohydrate from sugar rather than starch) with no protein intake can increase the movement of an amino acid called tryptophan into the brain. In turn this increases the production of a neurotransmitter called serotonin, which causes a natural sedation. Vegetarian and 'cleansing' diets of white rice, fruits and vegetables tend to produce the same sedative effect as high-sugar diets. Such diets can decrease your level of arousal, and make your right brain more accessible.

In residential workshops tea and coffee may be banned

as drugs. This also stops people having access to a natural stimulant to combat the sedative diet or techniques. In addition, such a ban can induce withdrawal symptoms in caffeine addicts that also may inhibit critical thinking.

Vegan diets, which eliminate all sources of animal protein and dairy foods so that the diet consists of cereals, fruits, vegetables and nuts, can change the pH balance (acidity) of the body. This is said to result in a subtle increase in carbon dioxide levels within the brain and a small decrease in available oxygen levels. It is thought such a situation makes it much easier for the brain to produce alpha waves, entering a state where it is more receptive to different beliefs and values.

A diet lower in fat and animal protein than normal, and with less tea and coffee, may be desirable for your health, and therefore can be successfully rationalised by the leader. However it should be remembered that extreme versions of such a diet may also affect your level of critical thinking, especially if the dietary change is a significant one for you and if you are under the circumstances of group psychological processes.

In cults the dietary regime can be so restrictive that malnutrition results.

USE OF LANGUAGE AND BODY CUES

Extensive research into the use of language in psychological therapy has led to the development of many exciting, highly effective but subtle techniques that can be used to help people resolve past traumas and conflicts, modify beliefs and change behaviour. The techniques are often combined with an analysis of subtle body cues being given by the subject, which reveal how he or she is feeling and processing information.

This combined use of language and body cues is commonly called neuro-linguistic programming (NLP). It often uses trances to enhance its effectiveness. It was developed in the early 1970s from systematic research by psychologists Virginia Satir, Milton Erikson and Fritz Perls. The techniques were further developed and popularised by John Grindler (a linguist) and Richard Bandler (a mathematician), as a means of changing behaviour and beliefs, particularly in marketing and sales situations where NLP has become a recognised sales technique.

One man who had completed extensive NLP training actually boasted to me that he was convinced he had been able to gain an extraordinary decision in his favour from a Family Law Court judge by his use of its techniques. In the first years of Australia's Family Law Court the judge, husband and wife and their representatives all sat around a table and tried to come to a mutually agreeable decision over both child custody and property settlement. Under such circumstances I have no doubt that what this man claimed was perfectly possible. He would have been close enough to 'read' the way that the judge (and the other people present) were processing information, and he could then use language that would influence the judge towards his way of thinking.

At the moment there are no restrictions on who may learn the techniques, who may teach them or under what circumstances they can be used. Some NLP trainers are qualified

psychologists themselves, who say they do screen participants in their courses, but many trainers have extremely
dubious qualifications – even in NLP, let alone any other
relevant field.

I have been told by cult members being groomed to
become leaders that they have attended NLP courses to learn
how to manipulate people effectively, particularly groups of
people. NLP means that someone may be deliberately
reading and interpreting subtle changes in your body
movements (such as where your eyes are focused) without
you being aware of it, in order to work out how you as an
individual process information and thus the language patterns (the kinds of words) that are most likely to change your
opinions, beliefs or behaviour.

NLP techniques are being increasingly used in business
(especially in sales) and politics to influence people. Under
the right circumstances language itself can be used to initiate
receptive states, by implanting suggestions that the listener
will change, or to enhance the effectiveness of programming
suggestions.

Embedded messages, either verbal or in print, can influence unconscious beliefs and behaviour. For instance, in
advertising brochures it is common to underline certain
words through the text. If these underlined words are
deliberately chosen to form a sentence, such as '*Buy a Ford
today*', this acts as a visual subliminal message on your
unconscious. Subliminal messages can also be conveyed on
audio tapes by emphasising certain words in the dialogue.

The semantic density of the language used (i.e. whether
it triggers an emotional, visual or aural response, or affects
all your senses at once) can dramatically change how many

people in an audience are influenced by what is being said. Advertisers aim for the same emotional effect when selling, rather than logic, because an emotional response is targeting the right side of your brain and your beliefs. For example, to a new customer the restaurant name 'Sizzler' taps into all their senses: sight, smell, hearing, taste, feeling. Compare your own response to that word with 'KFC', which has little semantic density – unless you have already been a customer of KFC and have certain images and feelings associated with your experiences. More new customers are likely to try Sizzler than KFC, as more people will be affected in more ways by this one word.

Similarly, compare your physiological and emotional responses to these alternative book titles: *The Role of Parents* and *The Power of Parents*. The second title touches many sensory cues and emotional responses, promoting immediate interest and arousal. The first creates little emotional effect and consequently causes a fairly neutral response and interest.

Health professionals like psychologists using these semantic techniques are governed by strict ethical guidelines and legal accountability. If as a community we don't wish NLP techniques to be restricted (and how could restrictions be enforced?), then perhaps we should at least insist that a subject is forewarned that the person they are dealing with is trained in these techniques, or using them.

As mentioned in Chapter 1, language can also be used as a confusional technique, to induce hypnosis and a non-critical acceptance of ideas and beliefs very quickly. This is usually done by having people listen to long sessions of information that may be contradictory or not make sense.

The left, critical brain quickly becomes exhausted trying to evaluate material logically that is in fact quite illogical and just gives up, 'blanking out'.

Language and words can also be used as post-hypnotic triggers to control behaviour. For instance, many cults have their own internal secret language for describing situations or people. If members of the group are showing signs of not conforming or not being compliant enough just the mention of these previously programmed words will act as triggers to elicit the desired behaviour.

DEPENDENCY

There is a common saying that 'adults are really just big children'. Many in our society (perhaps because all of us have imperfect parents!) appear not to have had our emotional needs in childhood adequately met. We often look like adults but have the needs of children.

Even if we are emotionally mature we are still social beings. We all need to feel we belong, that our life is important and has meaning, and that this is recognised by the community in some way. Most people get those feelings of belonging and importance initially through networks of family and friends, and then through their work.

Unfortunately in today's society individuals can easily become isolated, from family through marital breakdown and conflict, geographically isolated by the location of their work, and socially isolated by their working hours. If we had set out to design a society which least met the needs of people we really couldn't have done a better job!

Our need to be needed creates an interdependency between people which is healthy, if it is mutually respectful and balances the needs of both parties. In groups, courses and cults these needs can be abused so that the balance lies with the needs of the leader, not a healthy balance between the rights and needs of both parties. Too much power on one side of a relationship leads to too great dependency on the other.

Dependency can be created by groups in many ways, some of which have already been mentioned. Isolation from normal value references like work, family and friends, particularly if the person is being made tired, is very effective at producing dependency. Fatigue may be induced physically and emotionally – by lengthy sessions without adequate breaks, removal of watches or clocks, no access to radio, television and telephone, sleep deprivation or disturbed or interrupted sleep, intense physical exercise or work, uncomfortable conditions (cold or hot surroundings, uncomfortable seating), repetitive discussions or talks with no logical meaning or purpose. People may be actively discouraged from contacting their family or friends – even to let them know if they are late because the seminar is continuing over schedule.

Once dependent on the group, new beliefs are instilled. Gradually relationships with family, spouses and old friends become undermined as the new beliefs conflict with, or don't work well in, the old life. People are told that 'they have now outgrown' these old relationships and are operating at a 'higher level' so they will need to discard them.

However, if the new beliefs are *really* better, then they should enhance relationships and enable someone to *resolve* old conflicts and forgive family or others, not destroy or undermine relationships that previously had been important. Even if some relationship in their life does need ending or changing there are ways of doing this that are much more constructive than suddenly walking out, or blaming other people for their own problems and discontent.

CONFESSIONALS AND SECRETS

Usually very early in a seminar or group participants are encouraged to reveal something about themselves to other individuals, the group leader or the group as a whole. As soon as this is done (and there can be enormous pressure and psychological intimidation to do so), the person becomes very dependent on approval from the group and feels he must trust them as they now have one of his 'secrets'. Even if only one person is made to reveal or confess an experience or emotion this immediately commits the members of the group to one other, as they have all shared a secret that people outside the group don't know. (Sometimes a stooge is used to start the process of self-revelation.)

Besides a secret revelation or confession, some secret technique, symbol or enlightening 'truth' may be revealed to the group to enhance the idea of belonging to some special, select group. (Remember the 'secret societies' and gangs you were in as a child?) Secrets are used to increase commitment to the group.

DISTRACTION

If a person is asking too many questions at seminars or courses, or appears to be undermining the power of the leader in some way (even if they just have a good sense of humour that others appreciate), then this person will need to be 'contained' and distracted from questioning what is happening. This may be done by isolating him or her from others during breaks. Followers attach themselves to the rebellious person and start conversations with them, sitting next to them or even surrounding them physically.

During breaks people who are alone are immediately engaged in conversation or an activity. The reason is that if your mind is constantly being occupied or challenged it becomes extremely difficult to critically evaluate or reflect on what is being said or done.

In cults 'thought stopping' is used as one of the most powerful ways to distract or stop any kind of negative evaluation or criticism of what is happening in the group or the beliefs being expounded. Thought stopping can be achieved by repeating a single word over and over, humming, chanting, meditating, focusing on intense physical activity or 'talking in tongues' – anything that makes it impossible for the person performing the action to critically evaluate the situation. Because the process becomes automatic eventually it means it is impossible for someone to think negatively about the group – they stop the thoughts.

In closed cults thought stopping can become an *automatic* response to any negative thoughts within just a few weeks. In more open cults and groups the same technique is used to deny negative emotions and thoughts by regular meetings to reinforce the new beliefs and attitudes, such as the weekly Amway meetings.

RITUALS

Rituals invoke structure into activities. If they are done at regular intervals they can give people a powerful sense of structure and security in their lives generally. They can also reinforce naturally occurring biorhythms in the body if done on a daily basis, or more frequently. Then if the rituals are missed or not completed properly they can seriously disrupt such biorhythms, causing real physical discomfort, such as disturbed sleep or bowel habits.

Because strict rules are used to regulate rituals they can also be excellent ways of invoking guilt if they are not adhered to or practised properly. They also act as distractions, perhaps from more important issues, and as a way of focusing attention in order to dampen critical thinking and induce hypnotic states. For example, in the serving of food or position of seating rituals may be used to reinforce who is important and who is not. Rituals that are repetitive (chanting and processions) are particularly hypnotic.

REJECTION

If a person persists in questioning or undermining the authority of the leader and what is being done then the leader may use ridicule, humiliation or deliberately pick an argument with him or her. The leader may also use humour against the dissident and get the group to make fun of or ridicule them. Overt rejection techniques tend to occur more in cults, whereas in personal development courses the same rejection is accomplished but in a more good-humoured, subtle way. The effect is the same – the person is effectively rejected by the group unless he or she complies.

In extreme cases – people who won't shut up or who are able to create doubts in others – the dissidents will be forced to leave and told that they are just 'not ready' to benefit. The implication is made that these people are stunted somehow in their emotional development, or pathologically rigid because they are not ready to accept a new set of beliefs blindly. Of course this is the classic 'blame the victim' way of shifting responsibility for deficiencies in the course away from the cult, course, or group and its guru and his beliefs, and on to the participant.

Don't fall for it!

FOUR

Who Is Vulnerable?

Under the right circumstances *anybody* is vulnerable to the techniques I have described, especially if they are attending a course or meeting where the techniques are being practised without giving informed consent. Informed consent entails subjects being warned that they will be put through a psychological process (possibly including various forms of hypnosis) with the aim of changing their beliefs, and that there may be negative and unpredictable outcomes under such circumstances.

It is dangerous to assume that because you are an adult, responsible for your own life, that this somehow makes you immune from being manipulated. I have heard well-educated, intelligent people rather smugly say that only fools or neurotics can be adversely affected by cults – but remember the Hamilton-Byrne sect discussed earlier which deliberately targeted well-educated professionals. In fact the most vulnerable people are those discontented with some aspect of their life, or going through a life crisis (such as job loss, bereavement or ill health), who have above-average intelligence and/or good concentration. People who have a strong need for intimacy in their life are also particularly vulnerable, as are those who are idealistic and disappointed in what society has to offer.

The general discontentment or life crisis these people are experiencing means that they are likely to be already operating at a higher-than-normal level of arousal. High arousal dampens the ability to think clearly or critically: for instance, if you panic in an exam you can't think straight and your mind goes blank. Such people are predisposed by their arousal to be susceptible to the mind-control techniques discussed in this book.

The first approach made by cults can be very subtle and cunning. In contrast, a personal development group may *appear* quite overt in its intentions. Generally speaking a potential recruit is invited by a friend, acquaintance or business associate to an 'information evening' of some sort, a meal or 'networking' meeting.

These information evenings are the first step in recruitment, and the targets are actually being processed before they have done more than read an advertisement or accepted an invitation. The information evenings about future courses can be crucial to the organisation's activities, as they screen out people who are less likely at this time in their lives to be vulnerable to the techniques, or who will be too critical. Potential troublemakers can be identified at information evenings and may be told the course is full when they apply. This means that when the group or course actually starts the people attending have already been through a selection process and have committed themselves by paying, so will therefore be less critical.

Although I have attended a number of these groups it has always been as an observer. Even though I do not have any factors in my life at the moment that make me particularly vulnerable I would never actively participate in such sessions without the leaders being appropriately qualified, even though I am aware of what they are doing. People who suspect they are depressed, have had a psychotic episode or who suffer from asthma can be particularly at risk as some of the psychological techniques used can trigger suicide attempts, schizophrenia or fatal asthma attacks.

Children and teenagers are extremely vulnerable to ideodynamic techniques, for as I explained earlier their ability to critically evaluate information is not fully developed, and children tend to have more accessible unconscious processes than adults anyway. Also, as children begin to discover who they are and separate from their parents, they can easily become confused between competing family, peer and community values and their own expectations. Developing emotionally as a teenager is very much involved with creating an individual, appropriate belief system and set of rules.

The attraction of cults and groups for many teenagers and young adults is that they provide a clearly defined role for members, in a highly structured lifestyle with a comforting set of rules. Superficially they can also provide what appears to be a total acceptance of the person (as long as he or she obeys the rules!), and emotional and physical support, but without the hassle of past family conflicts, responsibilities and competing siblings. Young people and adults who are idealistic, with high expectations of themselves and other adults, can be particularly vulnerable to cults and groups as they may feel constantly let down by the unpredictable nature of their family relationships and the inability of their immediate social circle to meet their needs.

It is often suggested that cults and groups substitute for family. However I think this is a misleading oversimplification. In real families parents have emotional, social and legal responsibilities towards their children and are accountable to the community for their actions, plus there are competing restraints on their time – earning a living and functioning in the world outside the family. Also in families there are constant emotional demands from different family members that must be balanced – spouses, other children or elderly grandparents. The nuclear family can be a pressure cooker of competing demands and stresses for all those dependent on it to meet their emotional and financial needs.

In cults, or the artificial environment of a weekend or evening seminar, all the hassles of practical family life are left behind – as well as anybody whom the participant may have difficulties with in relationships. This leaves them free to enjoy an environment of warm acceptance by others in a nice fuzzy glow. It also allows them to express their own particular perception of difficult relationships (which may be very distorted), unchallenged or balanced by the people whom they are having difficulty with.

The single biggest difference between relationships developed in cults and seminars, with a guru or leader, and those within a family is that unlike a real family the group has no moral or legal responsibility for its members, nor is it in any way accountable for its treatment of them. In other words the group, guru or master can have all the benefits of knowing someone (including their money and labour) without any of the hassles or responsibilities a family has.

If a member becomes too demanding or not compliant enough then the group just expels them without any negative consequences to itself. In real families it is extremely difficult to get rid of someone who is upsetting others or not obeying the rules! The 'love' experienced by people in groups and cults is an illusion as it is entirely conditional on the member behaving and conforming to very rigid values.

A worrying recent development has been the number of schools allowing various groups to operate within them, such as Christian fellowship, yoga teachers and charity fundraisers. Schools are being increasingly expected to cope with the emotional stresses and socio-economic hardship of their students at a time when education budgets are being slashed, teachers retrenched, and non-teaching support services curtailed. For school administrators and school councils it can become extremely attractive to allow various religious and youth 'fellowships' to operate within the school in a 'pastoral' or counselling capacity. Some groups present themselves as charities, getting the students involved in activities or competitions to raise money.

Schools must realise that the fact that an organisation is operating within a school or has rented school facilities immediately gives it a degree of respectability and credibility in the community, which some groups are quick to exploit in promoting themselves and fielding criticism. Any group within a school should be scrupulously vetted and have strict limitations placed on their activities. I am not saying that all such groups use unethical techniques to recruit students, or their parents, but it is a fact that some of them do.

FIVE

Case Histories

~~~~~~

The case histories presented here are accounts of experiences of individuals who have contacted me believing that the problems they were having were triggered by involvement with cults, personal development courses and various gurus. Although I have changed names to protect identities, I have chosen case histories that are consistent with other experiences relayed to me about the same groups.

'Pauline'
Member of cult.

Pauline became involved in a cult while doing a massage course being run by the 'nicest, most caring person'. In the massage course many of the techniques described in this book were used, but in a gentle, humorous way that at no time aroused her suspicions: eye focusing techniques, changes in levels of arousal, NLP language techniques and commitment.

Pauline was resolving a very messy divorce at the time and was having difficulties coping with her three young children as well as working. The massage teacher invited her home, where the children were immediately occupied by a number of 'house guests', and gave Pauline the first break and practical support she had experienced since her divorce.

Gradually she attended more and more courses run by the woman and her husband. Like many cults the husband and wife worked as a team – a bit like the nasty policeman and the nice policeman. In this case the wife was nice and the husband could be extremely disapproving and controlling. Pauline learned later that both husband and wife had been Orange People in America and India before coming back to Australia. She was actively encouraged to include the children in her activities with the group and when it was suggested she give up her job and 'work' for them she agreed.

Over the next six years she became totally dependent on the group, 'invested' money from the sale of her house in New Age electronic equipment for use by the cult, and was intermittently abused by the leader and then supported by the wife until she became totally confused and compliant.

She left the cult when she was told that the leader had selected her thirteen-year-old daughter as a wife to bear him more children. When she left she owned nothing and had no income. The single parent's pension she had been encouraged to get by the cult was taken by them in return for her and her children's keep. She was never paid for any of the work she did selling flowers and chocolates door-to-door. These were cash sales and Pauline is sure that none of the money that she or the twenty other sellers earned was declared to the taxation department.

Pauline's children had not been allowed to attend normal

schools and were educationally way behind their peers. On entering the cult the children had been pre-school and primary age. They had attended 'classes' run by a cult member who was an ex-secondary school teacher, but much of the time was spent on 'nature' activities and 'self development' rather than systematic learning of skills in reading and maths.

Pauline and her children went to live with her elderly mother. She contacted me by phone but refused proper professional help because she was so scared of reprisal from the cult. She told me that she planned to go interstate. Her mother rang me a few months later to tell me that Pauline had committed suicide. The grandmother said she was moving interstate to be with the children.

'Harry'
Attended a personal development course on how to improve his business skills. I spoke to Harry and his wife.

Harry was an extremely successful executive in a large company. He was ambitious, competitive and highly motivated, with a more than comfortable lifestyle, a happy marriage and three healthy children. He felt his relationships were reasonably good but he believed he had not met his father's expectations. Although he was extremely successful he thought he should be able to achieve more in business. (Harry's wife felt that her father-in-law was actually very loving and proud of his son, and that it was Harry's own expectations that were too high.)

The course Harry attended was to be run over a weekend,

with sessions planned for the Friday night, Saturday and Sunday. However the length of sessions became extended to the point where he had no sleep Friday night, and the sessions on the Saturday and Sunday continued very late into the night. Because of the distance from home and the lateness of the hour the sessions finished he ended up accepting an invitation to stay with one of the 'helpers' at the seminar rather than going home. He did not see his family from Friday morning before work until Monday night.

At the end of the seminar Harry was on an incredible high, which he attributed to the wonderful 'mind power' techniques he had learnt at the seminar. He felt he had no limitations, that he could see things much more clearly than other people (later he realised this was because he now tended to see things in black and white and very simplistically). He thought he knew far more than his boss and that the company was holding him back. He also now felt his family were 'limiting his potential', and that he had a responsibility to himself to take charge of his life and discard any relationships that were inhibiting his real potential.

Consequently when he arrived home on the Monday night he announced that he had really 'outgrown' his wife, that she couldn't possibly understand, and he was leaving – which he did. By the end of the week he had so angered and alienated all those he worked with by his superior attitude, and his constant irrational attempts to get his boss to change the company's policies, that he was sacked.

His new beliefs allowed him to rationalise this as 'meant to happen' and he felt he could now reach his true potential as a developer in property and a speculator in shares. According to the seminar's beliefs his positive attitude meant he had to succeed. However he started to feel some guilt about confidential company information he had divulged to people in the group.

One month later his wife was forced to freeze their assets as Harry had made reckless business and speculative ventures that threatened to wipe out all they owned.

As the high of the seminar wore off Harry became depressed and tearful, he had headaches and mild arthralgia (pain in his joints). He then enrolled in another course and temporarily felt better. Soon he was a seminar junkie, addicted to the highs he got in the seminar situation. He was constantly contacted by the group and encouraged to become more and more involved with them. Two years later Harry had spent $20 000 on seminars, his marriage had collapsed, he was nearly bankrupt and his children did not want to see him.

When Harry contacted me he had not worked for over twelve months and was only just beginning to put his life back together.

'Linda'

Sixteen years old, attended a naturopath and faith healer. She was suffering from bad acne that she thought was making her feel very depressed and anxious.

Linda was aware of feeling increasingly depressed and anxious. She was often tearful and was having difficulty with her school work. Her mother was concerned by her mood swings and took her to their GP, who was a very caring young doctor Linda found it easy to talk to.

It was assumed by Linda and the GP that she was probably depressed because of the condition of her skin. He wrote a script to help her acne but did not have the time or the expertise to delve more deeply into her problems. Although her skin got a little better her moods did not, and the mother took her to a naturopath who also advertised as a psychotherapist and hypnotherapist.

The naturopath used acupuncture and relaxation techniques on Linda. He also used *guided imagery and visualisation* to help her relax and to heal her skin. Unfortunately, because he had no training in psychology and his qualification in hypnotherapy was not from a proper professional organisation (in New South Wales anybody can run a hypnotherapy school, without any qualifications, and anybody can attend a course) he used language and visualisations that triggered memories and experiences in Linda's past.

Linda abreacted while with the naturopath, sobbing hysterically, tearing at her hair, choking and gasping. The naturopath told the mother that Linda was having a 'healing crisis' and she would now get better. Instead Linda got worse. She started having severe panic attacks, nightmares, emotional outbursts, fits of sobbing and reacted very badly to some teachers and to her boyfriend.

Linda's mother then brought her to me. It soon became apparent that the visualisation (walking along a beach) and the guided imagery that the naturopath had used had triggered very traumatic memories. When Linda was quite young she had been molested on a beach and in the sea by the boyfriend of the babysitter looking after her and her brothers. The molestation was repeated each time she went to the beach throughout one particular summer. She had never told anybody what had happened, and she had been physically threatened not to tell. Her relationship with her boyfriend had activated the unresolved experiences, leading to the anxiety and depression.

With one session using EMDR (see Chapter 7) Linda's problem was resolved and her acne suddenly and dramatically improved, without any medication.

'Richard'
Attended a residential course to improve his study habits.

Richard was a highly social sixteen-year-old from a very wealthy home. He attended an exclusive boys school, where his reports repeatedly commented on his above-average ability not being matched by an 'appropriate' attitude or performance. 'Richard is not achieving his potential nor working to his capacity', they would comment.

Richard's parents were extremely disappointed and he was very aware of this. Although wealthy, his parents expressed their feelings that they were wasting their money on such an expensive school. One of Richard's teachers recommended a 'wonderful' residential course that could completely change kids like Richard into hardworking, motivated students.

Richard and his parents were very enthusiastic about something that could change him so profoundly. Richard did the course – run by people with sales and marketing experience – and his parents and teachers were astounded at the change. He returned home extremely 'high', loving school and brimming with confidence. Initially his parents were extremely pleased. However, they then started to notice subtle changes in his attitudes to others that they did not like so much.

Previously Richard had been extremely conscious of his privileges and had been very active in social service programs at his school. He now thought that people who had health or socio-economic problems had them because 'that's the way they really want to be', and that such people 'don't have the right attitude to succeed' or be healthy. He became critical of his mother's life as a homemaker and unpaid volunteer for many charities. He told his mother she was wasting her time with such people and should be putting her considerable talents to use 'making millions'.

He also started to be quite sarcastic towards his younger sister, who had serious learning difficulties due to neurological problems caused by birth trauma. He told his sister if she really wanted to read she could, and she was simply not reading to get attention and manipulate the family.

Richard's teachers became concerned because he now had an overblown opinion of his own abilities and when his grades, although much better than they had been, were not brilliant he started blaming the teachers. After several months Richard left both school and home, saying he was too bright for school and his family were holding him back. At last contact he was living with friends or on the streets and not working. His parents were struggling to keep contact with him to maintain some kind of relationship.

His parents are convinced that the course he attended caused a dramatic shift in his values and now feel that it would have been better to have consulted a professional for advice in handling Richard's poor attitude to school. The mother commented that even though he was not a perfect student before attending the course he had been a wonderfully caring son, brother and friend to people. She is now left wondering whether her and her husband's obsession with school grades had blinded them to Richard's real strengths as a human being.

The attitude expressed by Richard – that people are in *total* control of their destiny, whatever circumstances life has dealt them – is common to all of the cults, groups and courses that people have complained to me about. This simplistic and politically dangerous attitude allows cult members to ignore or deny the role played by social factors, health and the genetic make-up someone is born with in the success or failure of their lives.

As a psychologist I would be the first to acknowledge that people usually have far more power over their lives and their emotions than they ever dreamed possible. In fact that's what I do – I teach people to use that power, *and realise its limitations*, given their responsibilities, commitments and situation.

The political implications of teaching people to believe they have complete power over their lives is that converts to this philosophy think society shouldn't have to bother with social security payments, public housing and health. Their 'logic' makes them believe that if someone needs these things – is sick or out of work – then it's their fault and nobody else has any responsibility to help, especially not the community.

If such attitudes are disseminated widely through the

community, particularly in business and government, we are in for an extremely violent era as those who are denied access to help when they genuinely need it, through appropriate community and government assistance, will instead start to grab what they can regardless of the law.

Availability of psychological help

The preceding case histories are typical of many experiences told to me and illustrate clearly the issues that have been discussed in this book – that each person was discontented with some aspect of their life, was looking for appropriate help and this was not readily available from properly trained and accountable sources. Each was therefore vulnerable, with catastrophic results.

From numerous discussions with participants in groups and cults, or those who have become followers of gurus and masters, I have realised that many became involved because they were unable to get appropriate help with their personal problems, or had illnesses that were resistant to conventional medical treatment. After a frustrating visit to their GP – who although perhaps a caring and helpful individual would not have the time nor the *appropriate* skills to deal with what they wanted to discuss – such people are then attracted to individuals or groups offering peace of mind, increased 'power' in their lives, or healing.

As a psychologist I find the number of people in need who could have been helped by just one session with a psychologist sad and frustrating, but because of the lack of real accessibility to psychologists in the community (in part caused by lack of adequate staffing of community health centres, lack of Medicare rebates for psychologists in

Australia, and the lack of any comprehensive, accessible health care scheme in America except for very expensive private treatment), patients start a merry-go-round of faith healers and gurus.

Initially these groups and individuals may appear cheaper than a professional (especially as they have no restrictions on what they can advertise and promise to do). However, because the methods they use encourage dependency and there is no one to complain to about them, or to check on what they are doing, people consulting them can find themselves spending ten times as much as it would have cost to get properly qualified help in the first place – and they then may need help to repair the psychological damage done.

Community health centres in Australia and public health centres in America employ psychologists, social workers and psychiatric nurses. They provide some excellent group programs and individual treatment, but there are just too few of them and their waiting lists are unrealistic. Although there are plenty of trained psychologists in our community the lack of Medicare rebates in Australia, and of a public health care system in America, means many people cannot access their skills. Psychiatric treatment, which is available under Australia's Medicare and at public hospitals in America, is usually totally inappropriate for resolving emotional and relationship issues. In New Zealand there are similar difficulties with really comprehensive access to psychologists. However, psychologists are more accessible to the general public in the United Kingdom.

In the current political climate of deregulation, no restrictive trade practices and increased competition, it is difficult to understand why the federal government in Australia allows psychiatrists to have such an extraordinary monopoly on mental health care, when research consistently shows that for many kinds of problems psychological treatment is more cost-efficient and effective in the long term. In America psychological treatment is as available under private insurance as psychiatric treatment.

SIX

Protecting Yourself

ACCOUNTABILITY

A recurring theme throughout this book is the issue of accountability by those practising psychological techniques – to the individuals seeking help, their families and to the wider community.

Cults and personal development groups, gurus and masters, are often very good at creating confusion and guilt in the community regarding the question of individual rights. In a democracy, society should not be apologetic or tentative about the fact that everybody, whether they like it or not, has responsibilities and is accountable to that community. For instance, children are not possessions and parents do not have the right to mistreat children, or to restrict their lives in ways that prevent the children developing skills that allow them to function in the wider community.

Where responsibilities are shirked, it is the community that often ends up having to patch up and pay for any damage, or loses out in ways such as productive work of its members. Society operates through co-operation, not by allowing individual desires to reign regardless of the consequences.

White colonists of America and Australasia have a terrible record in their treatment of their indigenous peoples, and consequent ongoing problems, but considering the extraordinary array of cultures now living together in Australia, America and New Zealand, we are tolerant of each other and each other's customs in a comparatively peaceful, accepting way. One of the reasons for this is that we try to balance individual freedom with the needs of the community in a very practical, commonsense way, for instance adopting compulsory wearing of seat belts in cars and imposing restrictions on smoking in public.

This comparative tolerance found in many Western cultures of diverse religions and beliefs is now being appallingly abused. Western societies generally are often viewed as 'easy pickings' and safe havens for the activities of parasitic groups and cults. Many of them come from overseas, actively playing on a tendency to see something coming from abroad as better than anything on offer in the local community.

Unfortunately in the past, some sections of the media (particularly television) have had a worrying tendency to accept the legitimacy of gurus, masters and course promoters coming from overseas and allowed them extensive media coverage. They did not ask relevant questions about who these people were, whether they had appropriate qualifications for what they were doing or what was the evidence for their claims. Coming from overseas these visitors were certainly not accountable to anyone! Thankfully this is now beginning to change due to our healthy scepticism.

As a community we have to decide whether we want

government policies that effectively allow literally anybody, without any accountability, to go poking around in people's unconscious, or whether we want to be a bit more choosey over who has access to our own and our children's psyches. After all, if your child had a brain tumour you would want to know that the person drilling holes in his or her skull was highly trained, skilled, registered and accountable for what he was doing – not just the local carpenter who had decided to set up shop as a surgeon, with no appropriate training, registration or accountability.

When considering attending any group or course, always check out how much accountability the guru, master or group has if something goes wrong.

APPROPRIATENESS OF QUALIFICATIONS

There are now many people setting up groups and residential retreats, running seminars and heading 'sessions' in personal growth, healing or individual treatments, who either have no qualifications at all or no appropriate qualifications. Lists of letters after someone's name, or pieces of official-looking paper lining their walls, does not automatically give people qualifications for what they are doing. Unqualified practitioners are not necessarily motivated by money: instead they may be getting an emotional buzz from helping vulnerable people, while some may be enjoying the power they have over people attending their sessions.

Often practitioners produce books and tapes that may contain lots of rather obvious, commonsense statements and seem harmless. But unless the person has a very good training and proper experience in hypnosis, a tape supposed to solve problems may not be scripted with proper safeguards and can actually increase anxiety in a listener, opening a Pandora's box of past issues that have been inadequately resolved.

Many tapes are said to contain the answers that sick people have discovered worked for them. This does not necessarily mean they will work for everybody, or anybody, else, even if the problem appears to be the same.

A myth circulated by many unqualified gurus, masters and leaders is that you, a participant in their seminar or course, have to reach into the dark cupboard of your mind, root out any terrible things that have happened in your past, face them consciously and then release them in an explosion of emotion, beating the floor and screaming. This is commonly seen in rebirthing sessions and 'healing' ceremonies. I suspect that one reason 'letting it all out' or having a 'healing crisis' is a popular notion with these groups is that they somehow have to justify the rather alarming reactions that occur when using highly sophisticated psychological techniques in a crude, uninformed and dangerous way.

Most gurus and leaders assume that what comes up from a person's subconscious during such sessions are memories of something that actually happened. *This is not necessarily the case*, but 'evidence' manufactured or exaggerated under hypnosis can give cults ammunition to destroy other relationships in the recruits' lives, thus making them more dependent.

Moreover, confronting hidden traumas (especially if they didn't actually happen as remembered) can do more harm than good. In the case of sexual and ritual abuse, or torture, there is a danger that confronting the conscious mind with such issues in an inappropriate way can leave the participant with a complete nervous breakdown or psychotic.

Therapy conducted by skilled, trained and legally accountable people is always conducted with the safety and integrity of the patient given the highest priority. What he or she can cope with consciously as well unconsciously is always taken into account. No one has to suffer emotional agony or a 'healing crisis' in order to change. If psychological techniques are used properly then displays of emotion and feelings will be expressed and felt in ways that are appropriate for that person's *overall* wellbeing.

It can be extremely difficult to work out just what are appropriate qualifications for the help that is being offered. First of all use common sense. If you want to help your child improve his or her performance at school then you should consult a special education teacher. A registered midwife recommended by the local public hospital will be qualified to teach ante-natal classes. Apply the same rules when you choose a seminar or course: someone offering 'natural birthing' through advertisements in the local paper should be checked out with the health department or local hospital (many groups attract members by playing on the emotions of first-time mothers-to-be in 'natural' ante-natal classes).

Generally speaking, it would be extremely unwise to attend a seminar or course if 'personal growth' is being offered unless the leader is a registered psychologist or psychiatrist (see also the following section 'Questions to ask'). It is not unusual to discover that the leaders have been involved in the Moonies, Orange People or some other cult.

INFORMED CONSENT

This is a crucial issue. In a situation where beliefs and information are being presented you will evaluate these more critically if you know that the presenters are using persuasive psychological methods. For instance, if a leader says he is going to use hypnosis you will be in a strong position to decide whether you want to accept or reject what is being said. If you are not told that hypnosis is being employed you will much more easily and uncritically accept what is being programmed. One problem is that many leaders have no idea of the significance of the techniques they use! They have developed their trade simply from observing what goes on in other groups and deciding to set up shop themselves. If leaders don't know they are practising hypnosis they won't tell you, so you can't give informed consent.

Some healers have been treated by a properly qualified health professional and think that this, plus their own suffering, qualifies them to help others! Unfortunately if people have had serious problems this can actually interfere with their ability to help others effectively, as it can be extremely difficult for them to realise that other people's similar symptoms or problems may have totally different origins and solutions to theirs.

The important thing is to find out as much as you possibly can about the leader and his or her methods, so that if you do participate then it is with informed consent, not because you have been denied adequate information to make an informed choice.

QUESTIONS TO ASK

- Who is running the course?
- Are they registered by the government in any way?
- Are they members of an appropriate and recognised professional body?
- What standing do such bodies have in the community?
- What qualifications do those running the course have?

A degree or diploma in psychology does not mean a person is a psychologist. Psychologists must have at least four years' academic training plus two more years' clinical training. However, most clinical and counselling psychologists seeing patients would have a minimum of 8–12 years' training and be eligible for membership of the Australian Psychological Society, the American Psychological Association or the British Psychological Society.

The title 'Dr' can be meaningless in terms of appropriate qualifications, particularly if the degree has been awarded overseas.

- Are the leader's qualifications appropriate for the course and *valid in the country where the course is operating*?

A dentist running a stress management course may not be appropriately qualified, nor a computer programmer running a detoxification clinic.

- What *legal* accountability do the course and leader have if something goes wrong?
- What are the specific aims of the course?
- What methods will be used?

Check against Chapter 3, the section on 'Techniques'. Also ask specifically if neuro-linguistic programming techniques are to be used.

- If technology of some kind is involved (e.g. tapes, electronic equipment or biofeedback equipment), what is the *independent* evidence that these work?
- Is the course complete in itself or do you have to go on to do other courses?
- Cost. What is the *total* cost? Can you pay at the end? If you are not happy will they refund your money?

Get as much information as you can about the course, seminar or group. If possible write to the organisation and get them to answer your queries in *writing*. Any legitimate and appropriately qualified person with legal accountability will be happy to answer your queries on paper. Groups that attempt to fob you off, accuse you of being suspicious, won't answer questions directly or try to get you to sign contracts should be checked out particularly carefully.

If you are considering taking a course contact the Ministry of Consumer Affairs in your state and see if there have been any complaints about it. Remember that just because nobody has complained officially does not mean the course is safe. Many groups regularly change their name to prevent records being kept on them, while people who wish to complain are often confused and discouraged by having been told that their problems with a course are due to their own inadequacy or 'resistance', rather than to the group's activities.

Ask Consumer Affairs about the evidence surrounding the reliability and effectiveness of any equipment, gadgetry, meters or tapes being used. Also ask about the bona fides of any professional organisations or governing bodies the group claim to belong to.

Checking out religions

The world's main religions and sects are extremely concerned about their global responsibilities. In 1993 over 120 representatives of religious groups from around the world signed a 'Declaration of Global Ethics' to guide the activities of their groups. This was an unprecedented agreement on what constitutes ethical behaviour. It endorsed respect for all life and individuality and condemned limitless exploitation of the environment, violence as a means of settling conflict (especially where religious beliefs are used as justification) and sexual discrimination.

A useful guide to the ideals of any religion you are thinking of joining would be to ask if your chosen religion supported and practised this global ethics agreement.

CONSULTING HEALTH PROFESSIONALS

Don't be misled that I am wary only of unorthodox practitioners of psychology, or that I believe all orthodox church groups and registered health professionals are automatically good for you. However respectable an organisation is, it is made up of potentially fallible human beings. When approaching a church or health professional for help you should still critically evaluate them – both as human beings and in terms of their professional skills. Regardless of how 'legitimate' they may be, if you are not comfortable with them or their techniques you should go elsewhere, and if necessary complain to the relevant authority.

SEVEN
Getting Help

~~~~~~

LOCAL RESOURCES

If you are feeling alone, vulnerable or unhappy, or if you are generally dissatisfied with your life and relationships in some way, then try to find *appropriate* help for your problem, although this can sometimes be difficult. It is worth contacting your local community health centre or the Community Development Officer at your town hall or shire offices for information on what is available in the area. Citizens' Advice Bureaus also keep lists of local resources and courses being run by qualified people. Public hospitals usually have some psychological services available.

If you still can't get help, can't afford a private psychologist and don't think a psychiatrist is appropriate, then go and see your local Federal Member of Parliament and demand to know why you can't see a psychologist under the public health care system.

'CULT AWARE'

If you or somebody close to you has been involved with a cult, group or guru and you want more information and help on exiting from cults and groups, then contact Cult Aware, Locked Bag 1000, Granville, NSW 2142, Australia, or The Cult Awareness Network, National Office, Suite 1173, 2421 West Pratt Boulevard, Chicago, Illinois 60645, USA. Cult Aware has evolved from concerned members of the public, former victims of cults and personal development groups, and health professionals, all wanting to raise public awareness of the problem. Cult Aware can provide names of people near you who will give you further information on professionals working in this area throughout Australia and America. The Catholic and Jewish religions have been increasingly concerned by the activities of cults and have their own networks of appropriate help.

The Cult Awareness Network in America can put you in touch with people called exit counsellors (previously known as deprogrammers). Cults have been particularly clever at criticising the activities of such deprogrammers, who treated people who had been 'kidnapped' back from cults by their families. Kidnapping the victim back is no longer considered the best approach.

Exit counsellors are not usually people with any formal qualifications in psychology. However they have found by experience that the most important tool needed to break through a cult's dogma and to show the victim the inconsistencies and illogical nature of the cult's beliefs, practices and actions is a profound and deep knowledge of the particular cult involved. Exit counsellors also need to have ready access to corroborating evidence to support what they are saying, such as court documents.

Any attempt to confront a member of a cult or group with the inconsistencies in the beliefs of the cult, and negative aspects about it, *must be done in an indirect way* – usually by talking about the methods and beliefs of *other* groups. Ideally it should only be attempted by an exit counsellor or under their strict guidance and supervision.

Kidnapping your child, particularly when he or she is legally an adult, is a very difficult thing to accomplish in practice. In America there has been an increasing willingness by courts to try to understand the concept of diminished responsibility in an adult who has been subjected to a cult's influence. However in Australia general ignorance within the community and the legal profession about mind-control techniques means the attitude of courts tends to be that cult members are consenting adults. I very much hope this will soon change, as it is just not true.

Families considering trying exit counselling should be warned that if it is attempted on someone who is not co-operative, and without the exit counsellor having a sufficient and intimate knowledge of the cult, then there is a danger that it will not only fail but it will commit the subject even more strongly to the cult. Modern exit counselling does not need to kidnap a person and then force change. Rather it employs a process of allowing and encouraging the person to develop sufficiently to want to leave because of their *own* doubts and needs.

What Families Can Do

Parents with no access to an exit counsellor may be able to do little except try at all costs to maintain positive contact of any sort with the child. When contact is made it should be totally non-judgemental of the child's lifestyle and beliefs. If the cult member deliberately tries to begin an argument about his or her life the parent must not get involved, as this is a common method cults use to drive a further wedge between a member and his or her family.

Be aware that the cult will do everything it can to run the parents down to the child and criticise everything you have ever done as a parent. Again try and use neutral responses to such attacks and be comfortable with the fact that *no* parent is perfect.

A typical cultist statement is: 'You always favoured the other kids. You emotionally abused me and that's why I'm screwed up.' A good neutral response would be: 'I'm sorry if that's the way you feel. I suppose I wasn't a perfect parent at times, I just did my best', *or* (if the accusation is actually true or half-true): 'You are quite right. I made some terrible mistakes as a parent, mistakes that I regret deeply. I can't undo what I did, but because I do love you I'm trying very hard to change.'

Responses like this must be made in a matter-of-fact way, *not in an emotional tone*. A neutral voice and a non-judgemental attitude are crucial in dealing with friends or family involved in groups or cults.

In closed cults, where all forms of mind-control techniques have been used intensely – emotional, physical, cognitive (thought processes) and behavioural – the victim tends to develop a dual personality, as a way of dealing with the extreme stress of the conflicting demands and expectations of the cult and his or her previous way of life. Hence cult members can appear to outsiders to switch in mid-sentence between their normal self and their cult self.

In contrast, open cults and personal development groups use more subtle and sophisticated techniques for control, and these do not necessarily pervade the recruit's lifestyle. Usually the cult member does not show clear patterns of personality changes, and his or her behaviour appears quite 'normal' to outsiders. This modifying of existing personality, rather than very obvious changes in behaviour, makes the task of helping a victim exit from an open rather than closed cult much more difficult, because those trying to help may become confused about whether they are helping someone to escape or denying them the right to choose their own lifestyle. In other words, the harm caused by being a member of an open cult *appears* less clear-cut and not so black and white as the results of being a member of a closed cult.

This is precisely why so many previously closed groups are becoming more open – it is far more difficult for members to leave open groups, and there is a high probability that they will recruit family and friends. In addition, the longer people can be kept involved the higher is the likelihood that their own children will be raised with the group's beliefs and values, thus ensuring successive generations of members and with them a decreasing possibility of intervention from outside.

If you want to help a family member exit from a group you must look at it as a long-term project over many months (or even years). It is vital that you keep a non-judgemental relationship with the victim and avoid confronting their beliefs or ridiculing what they say.

Remember, it is not their fault! They are victims of extremely powerful psychological techniques that anyone can be vulnerable to at different times in their lives. However, you do not have to agree with them either. Adopt a curious, objective approach and try and keep the person in contact with ideas, activities and friends they had before they became involved. Do not give them money but give practical objects such as clothing, tickets to shows you know their 'old self' would have enjoyed and food. Talk about old friends, acquaintances and family in a chatty, day-to-day way. Mention ordinary things happening in your life at the moment, funny instances, old pets they once had or that you are still caring for.

Other family members must not blame themselves for the situation. They must keep it in perspective, balanced with their other responsibilities and commitments.

However, I would urge anybody concerned about someone they know to seek expert guidance as *soon as possible*, as it is very easy to unwittingly make the situation worse! Also collect as much factual information as you possibly can about the group, its leaders and its activities. Talk to ex-members and their families. Start a dossier. All this information – particularly about *how* involved the person is, what level they are at and how much they know about the group (this can be surprisingly little!) – will be vital to an exit counsellor.

The recommendations just given provide only very general information. The permutations and combinations of what happens between cultists and seminar junkies and their families are infinite, and every situation will be individual. If you or your family is in this position then seek professional help on how to handle it.

HEALTH PROFESSIONALS

The techniques for changing beliefs and accessing unconscious processes discussed in this book are refinements of techniques used by man for thousands of years. In the last forty years, and particularly the last fifteen, there has been an explosion of research into techniques for creating fast, therapeutic change in people to help them resolve past traumas, relieve very distressing symptoms, maximise the body's capacity to heal itself and adopt more constructive behaviour patterns.

Ancient cultures (which often used much cruder forms of these techniques) had *extremely* stringent controls on who could use them, under what circumstances and on whom. We in Western cultures have failed to put any effective controls on the techniques, even though our research has led to far more powerful and efficient methods of accessing the unconscious being developed.

Sales and marketing entrepreneurs have been quick to jump on this research and extend it further so that we now have highly sophisticated, subtle and potentially dangerous techniques available for literally anybody to use, on anybody they choose, without the permission or knowledge of the people being targeted.

Health professionals are trained to use their skills under

strict ethical and legal conditions. They are therefore often just as ignorant as the general population of how these psychological techniques are being modified for use in a manipulative way. But a growing number of professionals are extremely concerned about the morality of subjects participating in psychological techniques without giving informed consent, and the consequent damage that can be done. Some are now using their skills to help people resolve their experiences and get on with their life.

If a person exiting from a cult is voluntarily seeking help the most powerful, safest and fastest technique I have found of doing this is EMDR (Eye Movement Desensitisation and Reprogramming). This technique has been developed by psychologists in the last five years. Interestingly, it appears to be an extremely similar but a much more sophisticated version of a technique used by ancient cultures.

EMDR works on the principle that initiating different types of eye movements can give extraordinary access to the brain's mechanisms of processing information. Such access can be used by pyschologists to desensitise past traumatic events and reprogram more constructive beliefs and behaviour. We are only just beginning to understand this technique and what it can do, but its potential appears awesome, not just for resolving past traumas but also in accessing the body's natural healing response. It is still not clear whether EMDR is actually a form of hypnosis or an entirely separate process. EMDR can only be used by specially trained psychologists and psychiatrists.

If you wish to contact a psychologist or psychiatrist working with victims of cults, ritual abuse or other groups then telephone or write to the Australian Psychological

Society, the American Psychological Association, the British Psychological Society or the Royal Australian and New Zealand College of Psychiatrists. These organisations can give you the names of professionals close to you. If you specifically want someone trained in EMDR you will need to state this in your request.

EIGHT

Whom Can You Complain To?

If you have a complaint about an individual or group, and you have parted with money or goods in return for their 'services', you can complain to the Ministry of Consumer Affairs in your state (addresses and telephone numbers can be found in the White Pages of the telephone directory).

Unfortunately I have found many people are fearful of reprisals if they make formal complaints. However, if complaints are not lodged it is extremely difficult for Consumer Affairs to warn other enquirers about these organisations, or to make recommendations to the government regarding any need for legislation. In addition, without complaints the groups continue to prosper, getting away with what they are doing and making them even less likely to care for the consequences of their actions. Many leaders I have spoken to actually laughed gleefully about the fact that they were not being made accountable.

If you suspect there has been an abuse of the practice of hypnosis in Australia then contact the Secretary, Australian Society of Hypnosis, c/o Austin Hospital, Heidelberg, Victoria 3084. Even if your state has no regulations about hypnosis at the moment you should still report such activities.

If you or your family have suffered emotional or physical health problems as a result of the activities of some group or individual then write to the Health Services Commissioner in your state (again, check the White Pages for contact information). Although the commissioner is only supposed to be responsible for registered health professionals it's about time people started letting his office know what unqualified people are getting up to! Also complain to your local Member of Parliament – both state and federal. If we are going to have a co-ordinated policy on abuse of pyschological methods our state and federal governments need to co-operate.

In the United States there are now hundreds of people suing organisations that they have been involved in for compensation. Group actions of this sort may in the end be one of the most powerful ways of limiting the activities of groups, as money is certainly their Achilles heel! Some victims have already won large compensation payouts. I strongly suggest that anyone who has been dam-aged – either personally or through a member of their family – should seek legal advice regarding appropriate compensation. Contact Cult Aware in Australia and The Cult Awareness Network in America for the names of solicitors interested in pursuing such legal actions.

NINE

Conclusion

~~~~~~

There is a tendency (sometimes justified) to dismiss complaints by one professional group against other professional groups, amateurs or alternative practitioners, as attempts to restrict competition unnecessarily. However, for some years the activities of amateurs and inappropriately qualified people have been *increasing* my work as a psychologist, not decreasing it!

Health professionals and other people appropriately qualified for what they do are not magically perfect, totally effective, infallible practitioners. There are plenty of qualified people in all sorts of areas that I wouldn't send my worst enemy to! Nor should any one particular group have a monopoly on how physical and emotional health problems are solved. But because of the potential damage that can be done by totally untrained practitioners, *which the community ultimately pays for,* I feel we do have a right to demand some supervision of their activities.

Multiculturalism in our society introduces a wonderful variety of beliefs, customs, attitudes and behaviour. But at some point a consensus of community values, expectations and standards of behaviour must be maintained and insisted upon. We should not apologise for the need to do this, nor should we feel guilty that the good of the community as a whole must ultimately override the 'right' of an individual to do anything he or she likes.

Children are individuals that society has to make special rules for. They are not possessions owned by parents or particular groups. Their rights can only be protected if their care givers are answerable to community standards and expectations in terms of the physical and emotional treatment they provide, the beliefs they teach, the educational opportunities they allow and the children's interaction with the wider community. By allowing community needs and standards to be confused with the myth of individual freedom (a myth as ultimate individual freedom simply restricts the freedom of others) we set the stage for cults and groups to operate with the freedom to physically and emotionally abuse both children and adults. The cults are protected by their isolation and our woolly thinking.

In our society the first priority must be the needs of the community as a whole. Individual rights should be a huge consideration when establishing community standards, but they definitely must be the second priority. It is becoming particularly urgent to gain a clear consensus understanding of our priorities, as maverick groups are now making a deliberate push into business, politics, the public service and education. Unless we recognise their pernicious and insidious danger and combat it **we risk jeopardising the very foundations of our democratic way of life.**

Because of the sophisticated nature of the psychological techniques they are using they must be made at least as accountable as other business or health service organisations in our community. It is also vital to recognise that the groups are deliberately lobbying politicians and gaining political influence at local, state and federal levels. We must start to insist that politicians and political parties declare their financial supporters if we are going to be able to make informed choices over who wields power in our country.

Finally, this book is a plea for government legislation to control the use of psychological techniques by unregistered and untrained individuals. At the moment in Western countries like Australia and America the laws governing who can go rummaging around in your unconscious are in a big mess.

I realise that demanding strict supervision of anybody practising any form of psychology can have the opposite effect to that intended. Non-professionals do not admit to using psychology. Thus a situation is now developing where the only people who are open to scrutiny, are accountable for their actions and have restrictions placed on their activities, are those with training and registration; anyone else can do what they like. This is quite ludicrous!

Society spends considerable effort to keep adequate control of registered people and organisations with appropriate credentials. Why should we let any Tom, Dick or Harry set up with no restrictions at all? Do we really want to let anybody at all dabble in our unconscious without our permission?

If we are not prepared to bite the bullet and demand accountability from individuals and groups using these psychological techniques, then we at least have to insist on intensive consumer education so that people who do participate do so with informed consent.

I hope my book has made a start on such consumer education!

Helpful Organisations

Australia	Cult Aware Locked Bag 1000 Granville NSW 2142 Australia
Canada	Council On Mind Abuse (COMA) Box 575, Station Z Toronto, Ontario Canada M5N 2Z6
Denmark	Dialog Center International Katrinebjergve 46 DK-8200 Aarhus N Denmark
Eire	Irish Family Foundation Box 1628 Balls Bridge Dublin 4 Eire

France	Association pour la Defence de la Famille et l'Individu (ADFI) 4 Rue Flechier 75009 Paris France
Germany	Elterninitiative gegen psychische Abhangigkeit und religiosen Extremismus Postfach 30 33 25 1000 Berlin 30 BRD Germany
Israel	Concerned Parents Box 1806 Haifa Israel
Spain	Pro Juventud Aribau 226 08006 Barcelona Spain
UK	Family Action Information & Rescue (FAIR) BCM Box 3535 PO BOX 12 London WC1N 3XX UK

USA

Cult Awareness Network (CAN)
National Office
2421 West Pratt Blvd, Suite 1173
Chicago, Illinois 60645
USA

Bibliography

ANDERSON, Kevin Victor, Report of the Board of Inquiry into Scientology, Victoria, Government Printer, Melbourne, 1965

ANDRES, Rachel and LANE, James, eds, *Cults and Consequences: The Definitive Handbook*, Jewish Federation of Greater Los Angeles, Los Angeles, 1988

ATACK, Jon, *A Piece of Blue Sky – Scientology, Dianetics and L. Ron Hubbard Exposed*, Carol Publishing Group, New York, 1990

BAGINSKI, Bodo and SHARAMON, Shalila, *Reiki: Universal Life Energy*, Life Rhythm, California, 1988

BANDLER, Richard and GRINDER, John, *Frogs into Princes: Neurolinguistic Programming*, Real People Press, New York, 1979

BECK, Aron and EMERY, Gary, *Anxiety Disorders and Phobias: A Cognitive Perspective*, Basic Books Inc Publishers, New York, 1985

BELFRAGE, Sally, *Flowers of Emptiness: Reflections on an Ashram*, Seaview Books, New York, 1980

BOETTCHER, Robert, *Gifts of Deceit – Sun Myung Moon, Tongsun Park and the Korean Scandal*, Holt Rinehart & Winston, New York, 1980

BROWN, Barbara, *Stress and the Art of Biofeedback*, Bantam Books, New York, 1978

BURROWS, Graham and DENNERSTEIN Lorraine, eds, *Handbook of Hypnosis and Psychosomatic Medicine*, Elsevier Science Publications, Amsterdam, 1988

CADE, Maxwell and COXHEAD, Nona, *The Awakened Mind*, Delacorte Press, New York, 1979

CHURCH OF SCIENTOLOGY STAFF, *What is Scientology?*, Bridge Publications, Los Angeles, 1992

CLEVELAND, Bernard, *Master Teaching Techniques*, The Connecting Link Press, Lawrenceville, Georgia, 1987

CORYDON, Bent and HUBBARD, L. Ron Jr., *L. Ron Hubbard: Messiah or Madman?*, Lyle Stuart, Secaucus, New Jersey, 1987

DANER, Francine Jeane, *The American Children of Krishna: A Study of the Hare Krishna Movement*, Holt Rinehart & Winston, New York, 1976

DAVIS, Deborah Berg, *The Children of God: The Inside Story*, Zondervan, Grand Rapids, Michigan, 1984

DRURY, Neville, *The Elements of Sharmanism*, Aquarian, Wellingborough, UK, 1989

ELLIS, Albert, *Reason and Emotion in Psychotherapy*, Citadel Press, Secaucus, New Jersey, 1962

FREED, Josh, *Moonwebs: Journey into the Mind of a Cult*, Dorset, Toronto, Ontario, 1980

GRINDER, John, and BANDLER, Richard, *Trance – Formations – Neurolinguistic Programming and the Structure of Hypnosis*, Real People Press, New York, 1981

HAMMOND, D. Corydon, *Handbook of Hypnotic Suggestions and Metaphors*, Norton, New York, 1990

HASSAN, Steven, *Combating Cult Mind Control*, Park Street Press, Rochester, Vermont, 1988, 1990

HEFTMANN, Erica, *Dark Side of the Moonies*, Penguin, Melbourne, 1982

JENSON, Eric, *Super-Teaching*, Turning Point, California, 1988

JOHNSON, Joan, *The Cult Movement*, Franklin Watts, New York, 1984

JUNG, C.G., *Psychology and the East*, Ark, London, 1986

——, *Psychology and the Occult*, Ark, London, 1987

KING, Francis, *Witchcraft and Demonology*, Crescent Books, New York, 1991

LAZARUS, A., *Psychiatric Problems Precipitated by Transcendental Meditation*, Psychological Reports, 1976

LURIA, Aleksandr, *The Working Brain*, Penguin, London, 1973

MILGRAM, Stanley, *Obedience to Authority*, Harper & Row, New York, 1974

MILLER, Russell, *Bare-Faced Messiah: The True Story of L. Ron Hubbard*, Michael Joseph, London, 1988

MOINE, Donald and HERD, John, *Modern Persuasion Strategies*, Prentice-Hall, New Jersey, 1984

MORGAN, Brian and MORGAN, Roberta, *Brainfood*, Michael Joseph, London, 1986

O'HANLON, William and HEXOM, Angela L., *An Uncommon Casebook*, Norton, New York, 1990

OSTRANDER, Sheila and SCHROEDER, Lyn, *Superlearning*, Sphere, London, 1981

PATRICK, Ted with DULACK, Tom, *Let Our Children Go!*, E.P. Dutton, New York, 1976

PERSINGER, Michael A., CARREY, Normand J. and SUESS, Lynn A., *TM and Cult Mania*, Christopher Publishing House, North Quincy, Massachusetts, 1980

RANDI, James, *The Faith Healers*, Prometheus Books, Buffalo, New York, 1989

REED, David, *Jehovah's Witnesses: Answered Verse by Verse*, Baker Book House, Grand Rapids, Michigan, 1986

REICH, Wilhelm, *The Mass Psychology of Fascism*, Pocket Books, New York, 1976

REITERMAN, Tim and JACOBS, John, *Raven: The Untold Story of the Rev. Jim Jones and His People*, Dutton, New York, 1982

ROSE, Leonard with FITZGERALD, Peter, *Mirrors of the Mind*, McCulloch, Melbourne, 1989

ROSEN, Sydney, *My Voice Will Go With You*, Norton, New York, 1982

ROSSI, Ernest, *The Psychology of Mind-body Healing*, Norton, New York, 1988

ROSSI, Ernest and CHEEK, David, *Methods of Ideodynamic Healing in Hypnosis*, Norton, New York, 1988

RUSSELL, P., *The T.M. Technique*, Arkana, London, 1988

SAMWAYS, Louise, *Your Mindbody Energy*, Viking O'Neil, Melbourne, 1992

SARASWATI, Satyananda, *Asana, Pranayama Mudra Bandha*, 1969

SARGANT, William, *Battle for the Mind*, Pan, London, 1951, 1959

SAVANT, Marilyn vos, and FLEISCHER, Leonore, *Brain Power*, Piatkus, London, 1990

SHIRER, William, *The Rise and Fall of the Third Reich*, Fawcett, Greenwich, Connecticut, 1960

SINGER, Margaret, *Coming Out of the Cults*, *Psychology Today*, January 1979

SOSKIS, David, *Teaching Self-Hypnosis*, Norton, New York, 1986

STONER, Carroll and PARKE, Jo Anne, *All God's Children: The Cult Experience – Salvation and Slavery?*, Penguin, New York, 1979

STRELLEY, Kate, *The Ultimate Game: The Rise and Fall of Bhagwan Shree Rajneesh*, Harper & Row, New York, 1987

SWEARER, Donald, ed., *Secrets of the Lotus*, Macmillan, London, 1971

TERRY, Maury, *The Ultimate Evil*, Doubleday, New York, 1987

WALSH, Kevin, *Neuropsychology: A Clinical Approach*, Churchill Livingstone, Edinburgh, 1978

WALSH, Kevin, *Understanding Brain Damage*, Churchill Livingstone, Edinburgh, 1985

WILLIAMS, Robert and STOCKMEYER, John, *Unleashing the Right Side of the Brain*, Stephen Greene Press, Massachusetts, 1987

WILLIAMS, Linda, *Teaching for the Two Sided Mind*, Simon & Schuster, New York, 1986

WINGFIELD, Arthur and BYRNES, Dennis, *The Psychology of Human Memory*, Academic Press, New York, 1981

WURTMAN, Judith with DANBROT, Margaret, *Managing Your Mind and Mood Through Food*, Grafton, London, 1988

YANOFF, Morris, *Where is Joey? Lost Among the Hare Krishnas*, Swallow, Chicago, 1981

ZEIG, J.K., *Eriksonian Approaches to Hypnosis and Psychotherapy*, Brunner/Mazel, New York, 1982

Index